BirthCONTROL

"…I am a huge fan of P.G. Wodehouse, and some of your descriptive passages reminded me of him at his best (the wife's hand shooting up like a little pregnant Nazi; clumsily handing over the phone as if a bee had landed on [him], for example), which actually had the rare effect of making me laugh as I read…"

"…*BirthCONTROL* **is a hilarious recounting of the author's experience living out his wife's pregnancy. It made me think of UP ALL NIGHT or Parenthood, with a definite Woody Allen touch.**"

"…it is informative on the subject of pregnancy and the father's role, while actually being a dark, entertaining satire, it will probably appeal to quite a large demographic of the pregnant market (perhaps even rivaling the potential of the Perinealizer™)."

Birth**CONTROL**
A *Husband's* HONEST Account of Pregnancy

JAMES VAVASOUR

NEW YORK

BirthCONTROL
A Husband's HONEST Account of Pregnancy

Lyrics from "The Insulation" used with permission of Daniel Seim of Menomena. "The Insulation" appeared as a bonus track to the fourth album from Menomena, released on July 27, 2010 by Barsuk Records, in North America, and City Slang, in Europe.

ISBN 978-1-61448-340-3 paperback
ISBN 978-1-61448-341-0 eBook
Library of Congress Control Number: 2012945363

Morgan James Publishing
The Entrepreneurial Publisher
5 Penn Plaza, 23rd Floor
New York City, New York 10001
(212) 655-5470 office • (516) 908-4496 fax
www.MorganJamesPublishing.com

Author Photograph by:
Ashley Patranella

Cover Design by:
Rachel Lopez
www.r2cdesign.com

Interior Design by:
Bonnie Bushman
bonnie@caboodlegraphics.com

In an effort to support local communities, raise awareness and funds, Morgan James Publishing donates a percentage of all book sales for the life of each book to Habitat for Humanity Peninsula and Greater Williamsburg.

Get involved today, visit
www.MorganJamesBuilds.com.

To God, for everything.

To my wife, for our wonderful daughter and the amazing life we've built together.

To my daughter, for showing me love in its purest form.

CONTENTS

ACKNOWLEDGMENTS

I am grateful to my family and friends. For anyone included in this book, thank you for giving me a reason to laugh at myself. David Hancock and everyone Morgan James Publishing, thank you for believing in my book and giving me a chance. Kristina Holmes, thank you for generously pointing me to the perfect publisher. Sandi Gelles-Cole, thank you for being my trusted advisor and book doctor. Daniel Seim and Menomena, thank you for both your time and support. Amanda Tucker, thank you for your friendship and your council. Augusten Burroughs, thank you for your work, it is an inspiration. Liz Doyle, you were there from the beginning, thank you for your help and encouragement.

WEEK 3:

THE LATEX TISSUE

The good news was that, one way or another, this virility test was going to end in an orgasm. If I've learned anything in this life, it's that any outing guaranteed to end in an orgasm couldn't be a bad thing. I thought about what the place might look like. Positioned in the poshest part of town, a tall new building with gushing fountains centered underneath bright white letters with polished stainless steel trim, reading "LifeCorp." Walking through the automatic glass doors, I'd be hit with the scent of a candle cleverly mimicking the scent of freshly baked cinnamon buns.

Making my way through the magical sperm repository, I see a sexy blond administrator at the end of the lobby looking eager to take my name. She reaches under her desk, pulling out a stack of porn and shifting it invitingly towards me as I complete my paperwork. "Nice choice," she acknowledges as I made my selection. "This one is rarely picked, though it's definitely one of my personal favorites." Sometime later, after the shy glances from her no longer excite me, an equally attractive brunette nurse pokes her head around the corner. Grinning at me, like she just finished a long conversation about the hot guy in the lobby, "Ah... so *you* must be James."

She leads me back through the winding halls to a cubicle made from loosely placed bamboo dividers. It resembles a massage parlor, accented with a small table displaying a pot of fresh green tea and a neatly folded thick white cotton robe. She offers me a choice of five different lubricants, highlighting the finer qualities of each. I make my choice while she awkwardly hangs around just long enough to make me think she might stay. When she finally walks to the other side of the bamboo divider, I notice a thimble-sized see-through plastic cup on a small table. Smiling, I think how impressed they'll all be when I fill it to capacity.

I know what you're thinking, that's *exactly* how you imagined it. Well, it wasn't anything like that, not even close. You may ask, was there only a single porno magazine... Was it a *Playboy*? Even worse, a European *Maxim*? If only that was the case. No, the place I went was called LabTech and the experience was entirely different.

The journey began with giddy excitement. For the first time, a doctor's appointment wouldn't involve taking my blood pressure. There would be no tongue depressors. This would be like nothing I'd ever experienced, at least not in a doctor's office. I headed northwest, "Hmmm, Galleria is east, but no matter... I'm sure it's going be in some cool district of the city I've never seen before." Driving for several miles, I went from farm road to farm road, finally approaching what MapQuest stated as my destination. Pulling in, I saw a very unassuming building: a typical, sprawling, ugly, Texas, one story fake stucco strip mall that, as an architect, offended me deeply. I must be at the back entrance, judging by the distinct lack of fountains.

Inside, I was indeed greeted by a woman, but not of the variety that I had hoped for. She was blondish, with streaks of red and brown. Her hair was held in place with so much hairspray that it resembled cotton candy. She was thick in appearance and thin in manners.

She was surrounded by dusty silk plants. Green leaves spattered with purple trim—apparently a common silk variety, yet I've never seen its organic counterpart. She handed me a clipboard shockingly light in porn and heavy in forms. Completing it, I remained cautiously optimistic that something fantastic waited behind the large swinging aluminum doors to my left.

I tried to stare through the tiny Plexiglas windows encased in the doors, hoping to see some scrub-adorned *UFC* ring girls, *Hooters* waitresses, and *Tropicana* swimsuit models. Instead, all I saw were white walls spotted with teal and magenta painted doors.

After what felt like an eternity, the fingerprint-laden grocery store doors flew open. A nurse emerged that could best be described as a female version of Jim Norton, the balding guy on all the *Comedy Central Roasts*—except this version was wearing purple scrubs and a large grimace.

The nurse led me through the open magenta door leading to her office. There wasn't much inside: a desk and a grey plastic cart filled with *Sharpies* and what looked like sippy cups without the sippy part. She reached down and grabbed a single, ridiculously large sippy cup.

"Place the sample in this, put the cover on it, and bring it back. No lubrication is allowed. Go next door, close and lock the door and come back here when you are finished."

It took me a minute or two to process this information. The instructions were short and direct enough, but I was trying to wrap my head around the whole "no-lube" statement. Everything she said after those words were placed in the in-box of my brain, waiting their turn in queue.

There are two basic types of men in this world: the first comprises the normal population. These people get up in the morning and run hot water over a soft fresh facecloth. They place that warm, comforting facecloth on their face to open their pores. They calmly lather up a horsehair brush with shaving cream and evenly apply the moisturizing foam with aloe to their supple warm skin. It's usually around this point that they pull out a razor. The general rule of thumb on razors is that, if the razor has fewer blades than you have fingers, you probably live on a ranch. Either way, you run said razor under scalding hot water and begin shaving. Once finished, these men splash hot water on their faces, pat them dry and complete the process with face balm and a finishing mist of after-shave.

This brings us to the second category of men: masochists. Masochists get up, grab a rusty old disposable single blade razor from the top shelf in their medicine cabinet and begin tearing stubble and the topmost layers of skin from their faces. No product is needed, only limited amounts of cold water. Their face is left bleeding and raw. *These* people masturbate without lube.

Defeated, I took my sippy cup and went back into the hallway looking for the room the nurse had described. There was only one nearby door; it was the teal green door next to the nurse's office. Inside a virtually empty room waited, with a belly-button-high grey fabric cubical wall cutting it in half. There was nothing more than a single stool behind that half wall, and it was upholstered with dull magenta leather. On the nearest side there were built-in grey cabinets with grey laminate counter tops highlighted with, you guessed it, green and magenta flecks.

The sexiest thing in the room was the opened box of latex gloves resting on the counter with one limp glove waving from the top like a half drawn tissue. There certainly weren't any cups of green tea or bath robes to be found. Even worse, there was no sink, or mirror, or even a hook on the door. How could you not have a sink in a masturbation room? How was I going to clean up? I immediately realized that the whole room was most likely covered in a thin film from hundreds of men's cumulative "samples." This was a road I could not travel. My brain needed shutting off if I was ever going to have any chance of getting off. Back to the sink. Without a sink, what was I supposed to run wastefully in the background to cover up the sound of... you know? Damn it, this was going to take a while... no this was going to take painfully long. I desperately wanted to leave, pack up my penis and go, accepting failure in what might be my first fatherly act.

Four days and three hours later, only after sheer hunger and sleeplessness drove me to find the strength to ejaculate in the humongous sippy-cup, did I emerge. So, it may not have actually taken that long, but the cup was huge. Had there been a sink in that room, I would have added water to my "sample" just to hide my shame... ah, right, no sink—now it makes sense. Walking in to the nurse's office, I was blushing, dehydrated and ashamed. She pointed to the grey plastic cart and said, "Take a marker, write your name on the side of the cup and set it down there. You'll get the results back in a couple of weeks."

The days that followed my virility test brought me to the first pregnancy myth in a long list of untruths I would soon expose: planned pregnancy. Unless, of course, you simply meant pregnancy has a plan of its own. I would soon leave the comforting routines

I had always known, pulled along in the wake of a life I no longer controlled.

What the nurse and I didn't know was that we were both wasting our time. I had a whole other test being processed at that very moment, a cheaper, more accurate virility test: an ovulating uterus, specifically my wife's ovulating uterus.

WEEK 4:

BABY CAVE

One week later, my results came back in the form of a blue line. It should have been a lesson to me. Conception was defiant, caring nothing of our plans to start trying the following month.

I remember how the morning started. My wife, Ellen, told me that she thought she felt something going on in her ovaries and suggested she might be pregnant. Not possible, I thought. I haven't gotten my virility test results back yet. In my mind, I was sterile until a doctor told me otherwise.

For years, I'd been called a hypochondriac by my closest friends. They were wrong: I didn't invent problems. Symptoms were simply evaluated, and eventually I settled on what I felt was the most probable diagnosis. In this case, the evidence came about six years ago from an urologist's diagnosis: one functioning kidney and one non-functioning kidney. Basically, this meant one kidney was functioning correctly and one kidney was a giant dead sack of pee. I was told that it was probably "just a birth defect" and was nothing I needed to worry about. This news, of course, came a few moments too late, after the urologist, like a bloodhound, had already gone straight for my testicles. The good news was completely overlooked. Instead of moving on with my life, I choose to fixate on that very moment: the moment my testicles became a thing of interest to that urologist and somehow symptomatic of a dysfunctional kidney.

Thankfully, at the time, I at least had the wherewithal to enquire, "Why the sudden testicular obsession?" He went on to explain that kidney-related birth defects affect sexual development. This was vague and not particularly helpful to me, so I pulled out my laptop that evening and began a thorough investigation on WebMD. I found some particularly interesting information.

A kidney defect at birth could lead to restricted growth? Gary Coleman, for example, had kidney disease when he was born, which explains why he never grew any taller than four foot seven. I'm six foot four, 235lbs. Finding out I was one kidney away from being the white Arnold Jackson was pretty shocking to me.

Unlike Gary, my height was unaffected, my penis appeared adequate, and my testicles were verified by my urologist as reasonably placed and to scale. So, why was I so worried about being sterile? It was because I'd dated a lot of crazy girls. Not only had I dated them, I'd been in long term relationships with them and never had a single pregnancy scare. Not so shocking for a guy with all his organs—one could simply pass it off as good luck. However, once I'd established that I was one kidney away from micro-penis, I spent the next six years convincing myself that I had been robbed of functioning testicles. I grew to accept that I had placeholders serving no other purpose than to frame out my penis.

I was wrong. I wasn't sterile at all. I was the Greek god of semen. I was Testeclese. I had successfully impregnated my wife only weeks after she had stopped taking birth control pills. I felt joy, but also pity for my wife's exhausted and defeated body. Not because of the transition she would soon undergo, but for all the years her body must have struggled to fight off my powerful libido. Every cold, sinus infection, fever and back-ache she suffered since dating me was almost certainly a result of a weakened immune system from fighting off the constant threat of pregnancy. We were lucky she was able to defend against my super-sperm's will to impregnate as long as she had.

Ellen needed a doctor. Fortunately, we were only three miles away from her OBGYN, a proximity that served me well. It won me an argument when Ellen suggested we consider using a midwife to deliver. I convinced her that the midwife practice was too far away in city traffic. This was a much better argument than how I truly felt: midwives were un-American and Ellen was two hairy armpits and a midwife away from losing her passport.

Ellen and I met at the doctor's office later that week, both having left straight from work. Normally, I would puff-out my chest in a room full of women, but not here… there was no need. Nothing said "functional penis" like a husband accompanying his wife to a gynecologist's office. Before we knew it, Ellen's belly would puff-out enough for the both of us. We waited anxiously, imagining what we might see. Could the ultrasound already detect if we were going to have twins? I was pretty sure it couldn't detect the sex this early. The penis wouldn't be developed enough at this point, but you never know. Who knows how big my penis could have grown had it been supported by two functioning kidneys. Do *Pampers* even make diapers to accommodate something like that? *Pampers* Magnum. My thoughts were interrupted by the nurse, "Va-va-sour?"

We headed toward the room and, for once, it was exactly how I had imagined it. Maybe because my expectations were low, or more likely because I never wasted much time fantasizing about the inside of an OBGYN's office. We sat inside for a few minutes while the nurse exchanged pleasantries and asked my wife to de-robe.

This marked the end of my wife's body as I knew it. I imagine much in the same way a werewolf's husband might feel as his furry bride revealed herself on the first full moon after their wedding day. My wife's body morphed, but not into a hairy monster, howling as she roamed around aimlessly in the darkness, not yet anyway. But her vagina, once a beautiful place of magic and wonder, was only moments away from becoming a nine-month-long science experiment.

Ellen nervously sat back on the industrial strength thigh master, spreading her legs, as she bashfully pushed the thin paper robe down between them. Within seconds, there was a knock on the door and it popped open about a third of the way.

"Hello?"

Wow that was fast. I usually sat flipping through year old copies of *Country Living* for nearly a half an hour when I was at the doctor. Of course, I wasn't sitting alone in a room with my half naked wife, spread-eagle, in what was essentially the world greatest sex chair. Yeah, they'd better be fast.

"So what's going on?" the young, reasonably attractive, female doctor asked as she walked into the room.

My wife went on to disclose the results of our pregnancy test and how she'd been feeling. I didn't listen, I was preoccupied. As if compelled by some twisted gynecological instinct, the doctor's left hand shot out blindly and grabbed what could only be described as a slightly elongated *Nintendo Wii* controller. Simultaneously, with her right hand, she reached forward into a nearby tissue box and pulled out a loose condom. She then rolled the condom onto the joy-stick single-handedly. She even pinched the tip. Reaching for a nearby white tube, about the size of a *Pringles* can, she continued to engage Ellen. She squirted something that looked like a distant cousin of the blue filling from an icepack over the end of the condom-covered controller. Never breaking eye contact with my wife, she gave the *Wii* controller the smallest little hand-job. Before Ellen had time to react, the 1982 black and white 12" televisions to our left and right began to display an indecipherable grayish blur.

"Yep, there it is. It's early, but you are pregnant."

I peered deeply at the screen for anything that looked remotely like a penis.

"See that black dot? That's the hole in the uterus where the egg's implanted itself to develop."

Oh my God, I thought. That little hole is our baby.

WEEKS 5 TO 12:

NO SIGN
OF A PENIS

As the weeks passed, we began the futile but mandatory expecting parent quest for knowledge. We researched the big items like "What should Ellen avoid during pregnancy?" As it turned out, the simpler question may have been "What in the hell *can* Ellen do during pregnancy?" We knew the obvious stuff like alcohol, sushi, roller-derby and poison. But did you know that pineapple, eggplant, and small dogs with flea meds could also be dangerous? We soon learned that catalysts for any number of birth defects hid behind every corner.

Any and all research we began opened Pandora's Box of further research, all written by authors waiting to tell you whatever you wanted to hear for $22 and a *Barnes and Noble* book card. Books were clearly organized by motif, with words like "Natural", "Midwife", "Homebirth", and "Dr's Guide." For the record, none of our books had "Easy" in the title. Most of the knowledge Ellen sought led you to believe that "Easy" was for venomous unfit mothers frantically seeking any way out parenthood.

Despite all of these imminent threats, our baby appeared to be progressing well. Our next doctor's visit pointed towards a healthy pregnancy. We had another ultrasound and the same 1982 black and white 12" televisions revealed our cute little hole had now evolved into something resembling a peanut, our Peanut. Proudly, I asked for a picture, and the OBGYN obliged with a thin heat activated printout that closely resembled a receipt. This particular receipt, I was guessing, pretty much summed up every purchase I was going to make for the next eighteen years.

Our next appointment would be our Spina Bifida, Down syndrome and general anatomy ultrasound appointment, and it would be in the newest of a recent boom of medical buildings to pop up in our neighborhood. Thirty-five stories high, the intricate blue glass crown on top excited me. After a quick internet search, I learned that the crown was actually an artist's 3-dimensional rendition of the hospitals beacon logo, which, by this city's standards, may as well have been the Guggenheim.

A futuristic bridge from the latest *Star Trek* Federation Starship came to mind when I tried visualizing how the lobby might look. I was already mapping out the conversation I would use entertain Ellen while we waited, acting like some distant relative from the future. "Ell279, can you believe our organic ancestors traveled here by petroleum motored wheel-ships hundreds of years ago." In my best robot voice, I would continue, "They had children when they themselves were merely thirty years old. I am so glad we waited until we were two hundred, it is good to have children while my second cloned head is still so young."

The building's interior didn't deliver on the exterior's promise. The understated lobby led to a single bank of elevators at the back. The twenty-third floor looked like a bad Las Vegas casino buffet. Light golden-stained wooden tables and cheaply upholstered grey chairs, printed with random blue and red brush strokes, lined the center of the waiting room. Facing them, an *IKEA* grade check-in counter hailed back to the early 90's. In the corner laid the typical, colorful, twisted wire abacus-looking children's toy that came standard with any medical office. I dismissed such toys, like I dismissed *Nickleback* on modern rock radio, as being just dumb enough to have mass market appeal.

My excitement was fading. We sat in the waiting room for nearly forty five minutes without peeing or eating, which was a pretty big accomplishment. Alas, Peanut had had enough and decided to man the helm, steering Ellen's avatar to the front desk. I could imagine the little voice in her head "Mother! Seek food! Do as I command!" Within a few minutes, Ellen returned eating the stack of peanut butter crackers she had shamelessly begged from the women at the front desk. It was amazing, the charity people offered to pregnant women. Men would leap to abandon their chairs in packed restaurants and grocery stores even had pregnancy parking spots placed closer to the door than the handicapped ones. However, I'd noticed that pregnancy parking spots were usually occupied by non-pregnant over-weight, lazy bastards that could have benefited from a little exercise.

If it hadn't been so hot, I would have tried to convince Ellen to relax in the nicely shaded corner of an overpass. Nobody with a conscience could drive past a pregnant young woman at the corner of an intersection without handing over everything in their wallet. All she would need to do is phone in some weak attempt at a sign and prop it up against her feet. It wouldn't even need to be creative. The operation could be run with no overhead beyond the purchase of a Sharpie. "Pregnant and alone please help", would be more than adequate, or, for an even bigger pay-off, "Taliban rape baby from serving in Afghanistan. God bless America." Personally, the funny ones always tickled my philanthropic fancy. However "Why lie? I need a beer." probably wouldn't go over well in this case.

From what I'd been reading, begging wasn't the only way to cash in on pregnancy. Milk banks offered milk, at exuberant prices, for those who couldn't produce their own. It made more sense when Ellen read to me that "…human breast milk was the most efficient food on earth." I wondered if *Smoothie King* had ever investigated the breast milk smoothie. Was there a black market for human breast milk? Maybe there was some strange breast milk fetish of which I wasn't aware. It certainly seemed plausible and could have mass appeal to the more health-conscious deviant community. Think about it: the perfect perversion with none of the nasty side effects that might accompany asphyxiation or cutting. If anything, you might even be better for it.

It wouldn't work for me personally. I felt that breast feeding was a distant relative of cannibalism. Though I might consider it should I ever get caught in the Andes after a nasty plane crash. When thinking of those whose interest would be piqued, sleazy skinny guys with milk mustaches came to mind. Hanging around the parking lots of milk banks, badgering small chested mothers whose milk hadn't come in. "Buy me a 40-ouncer while your inside," they'd whisper as they flashed a large wad of cash. As farfetched as this may be, breast milk was in high demand and went for as much as five dollars per ounce.

We had no less than four friends currently breastfeeding, and I smelled a business opportunity. I would love nothing more than to be a stay-at-home milk pimp. Sure, I would have my low tier stuff that changed hands for a fiver, milk from moms that ate fast food and drank *Coke*. But for those with discerning tastes, I would have my top shelf breast milk, the good stuff that sold for more per ounce than Iranian saffron. You could find me outside of high end baby boutiques; I'd pull out my wallet and thumb through the pictures until I came to an attractive young mother. "See her? She drinks nothing but bottled water sprung from the French Alps. She eats wild-caught fish, and otherwise she's a vegetarian. For dessert she eats only organic berries, the five variety blend leave the milk with a wonderfully fruity finish," I'd pull out a doll sized plastic baby bottle, "Hey, don't take my word for it. Taste for yourself…"

The nurse walked into the lobby and nervously stuttered, "Ba-Va-Sour?" We got up and followed her to the examination room. As we made our way, we could hear the gut wrenching sound of a sobbing couple not too far down the hall. As the nurse closed the door behind us she explained, "We don't always have good news. That's the hard part of this job. Usually everything's fine, but sometimes it isn't. That's why we are running so late today, I'm sorry about the wait." Suddenly, two hours of waiting while eating peanut butter crackers and watching daytime television didn't seem so bad.

As she sat Ellen back into the chair for her exam, we finally began to see evidence that the building was brand new. Small color flat panel televisions replaced the dated black and white televisions of our OBGYN's office. Once the test began, the technician explained that we were looking for a small pocket of fluid on the back of the baby's neck. The depth across should fall somewhere between one and three millimeters, measurements greater than that are linked to Down syndrome. I understood "millimeters" because I was Canadian. To my American wife, this was a meaningless infinitely small measurement of no consequence. Fortunately, our baby landed right in the middle. The technician continued to point out the spine, heart, legs, and arms. Many of the main organs were also visible; however, one key organ was not being addressed to my satisfaction.

"Any sign of a penis or a vagina?" I asked.

"Not yet, but you should be able to identify the sex in a couple of weeks."

I don't quite remember what I said at the time, but I am guessing I made some uninspired "I have a big penis" joke. I'm sure I probably suggested that the technician clearly hadn't been looking hard enough. Ellen probably gave an embarrassed laugh and rolled her eyes. What I really remember was not being able to let go of the couple down the hall. I dwelled on Ellen's every choice in the days that followed, everything from organic meals to the safety of seatbelts. Already my paternal instincts and insecurities left me second guessing whether we had been doing enough to protect our little peanut.

WEEKS 12 TO 20:

THE CHEATING
STRIPPER

The little things you took for granted as constants began to change once "we" were pregnant. For example, Ellen's nipples, once the soft pink starting line of foreplay and stimulation center of the breast became our own little *National Geographic* special. During pregnancy the nipples grew darker and larger for the baby to spot, like some half blind hairless koala bear pulling itself up a eucalyptus tree looking for a thick fleshy leaf.

Change wasn't only limited to Ellen's body. Our relationship also changed: we began to bicker much more often. It seemed like every time we got in the car there was a new debate. Of course, I was at a disadvantage, my podium barreled down the freeway at seventy miles per hour. It navigated roads, steered away from cars, children and brick walls all while under the onslaught of loaded questions from an opponent who had been poked with the "Sharp Hormone Stick of Crazy" for the past few months. Normally, the debate was limited strictly by the length of our journey. The only exception was when Ellen deemed it necessary to extend the closing remarks into the parking lot of our destination while onlookers rejoiced in watching me be humiliated.

As an example, one day's test of intellectual agility revolved around the subject of "girl names." Fortunately, this was less volatile than most of our previous debates because, on the subject of names, I had little to no impact on the decision.

"How about Ruby?" Ellen asked.

"Ruby was the name of the cheating wife of a crippled Vietnam War Vet in a song sung by countless artists including Kenny Rogers, Cake and the Killers. Do you really want to name our little girl Ruby?"

"I like it," she would say, like I hadn't even spoken. "How about Electra?"

"What? Ruby wasn't slutty enough, now she has to be Electra? Why not just name her Mercedes or Jade?"

"I like it," she whispered as she stared out the passenger side window in an effort to hide her radiating joy as she gouged away any possibility of me living over 55. "What do you think of Abigail?"

"Too much like Gail..." I said, "...the stripper in *Carlito's Way*. Plus, people would call her "A-Big-Gal Vavasour" or even worse "A-Big-Gal Dinosaur""

"I like it. Sophia is nice too, it's classic and Biblical."

Judging by this conversation alone, one might think "Jeez, why didn't he just suggest something instead of being critical of every name she proposed." Well, I did. My name selections were presented via email in list form, twenty to thirty names at a time. Each name was categorized to please Ellen under either "Greek" "Arabic" "Biblical" or "Names I Just Like", a virtual ethnic baby name database. All of the names on my list had to be painstakingly analyzed before making the cut. I needed to protect our child from the endless ridicule I received growing up. With a last name like Vavasour, the first name was destined to be combined with "a-saurus", so I needed to at least give them a solid first name to work with. Two to three times a week I would present my newest list, praying that at least one of my preferred names would please her Royal Hormoness, but alas they never did.

No matter the effort, each new list was an exercise in futility; it was hours of wasted research in preparation for inevitable rejection. I'd even considered compiling a list of the names she fixated on for no other reason than to demonstrate her blind rejection of anything I presented. But it was too early. She needed more time to stew in her hormonal broth before I could make such a bold move. It became such a source of stress that I would virtually throw a printed list across the cab of our truck waiting for its ultimate fate, complete and utter dismissal. She would painfully mouth the names I presented to her, like Harry Potter struggling to say "Voldemort" and then gaze thoughtfully out the window at the trees as they whipped by.

"Hmmm... I think I still prefer Abigail," she would offer, like there was still some negotiating room. Finally, after hours of painful faux deliberation, she would once again begin the launch sequence to her missile of torment: "Ruby, Electra, Abigail, Sophia."

"Did I tell you I had a dream once that I had a daughter named Abigail?" she would ask time and time again, like God had already settled on our child's name when Ellen was eight.

"Yes, Ellen, you've told me about a hundred times. Did I tell you I thought of an awesome boys name in church last Sunday? Hear me out... Urijah!"

"Hmmm… I actually like that name," Ellen shockingly responded. "I think we may have agreed on a boy's name. See, we're making progress."

"It's a girl!" the doctor said with a big smile as she rolled the ultrasound around, bringing the image of our baby's skinny little bottom into the foreground while striking the print key. Ellen looked at me and smiled with an excitement I've rarely seen her express. My eyes jumped back and forth between her and the monitors in disbelief.

How can we be sure, I wondered? "Can you see the kidneys?" I asked, hoping we were not in fact witnessing a kidney-less boy with a micro-penis?

"There they are, back here. I can tell because the bladder is full. It looks as if she's producing her own urine," the doctor said as she switched views to our little girl's abdomen.

I was elated; I think I had secretly hoped for a little girl. Little girls were for daddies. My role in all of this suddenly deepened. Our little Peanut had just become Abigail Sophia Vavasour.

Little did the nurse know how the words "It's a girl" triggered the neurons in my brain. Neurons that, until now, had sat quivering in anticipation for the baby switch to move from "Peanut" to either the "Girl" or "Boy" position. Within two days of our appointment, I had prepared a nursery folder for Ellen. Several mural options were printed in color, all involving trees… everything from literal and lush to single color abstracts. I had images of various types of crown molding, tree branch curtain rods and shades-of-pink wall colors. I loved having a project. This project in particular offered me something more: a voice in our pregnancy. It was something to call my own, but most importantly, it was something I could give to Abby.

"Hmmm… the room is already painted blue, why don't we leave it?" Ellen said, having clearly felt that this would be the most rewarding feedback she could offer.

It took me a while to process her question. She was aware that we were having a girl, I was sure of that. I wondered for a second if maybe she was joking, but Ellen doesn't joke. I continued to look for any sign that I had misunderstood. I slowly and quietly whispered the word "Blue" while looking at her. She offered no reaction and brought me no closer to understanding her position. I was pretty much pro everything when it came to the gay community: personally, I believed that everyone in the world was varying degrees of gay and that "straight" didn't actually exist outside of a philosophy. Nonetheless, I didn't see the need to somehow throw our little girl into a room solely designed to initiate "Sequence Gender Confusion". Not to mention it undid everything I had imagined from the moment "Girl" was uttered and a fuzzy pink blanket had fallen across the world.

The negotiation took several hours, but I eventually managed to convince her that perhaps green would be some form of common ground. Now that we had agreed on a color, I could proceed to *Lowes* to find the pinkest shade of green they offered. Fortunately, the rest of the negotiation went much faster. I felt that I could sneak injections of girlishness throughout the project without drawing too much attention from Ellen. Even if she did figure it out after the big reveal, she was probably already too pregnant to do anything about it.

Within minutes of establishing a way forward, I was out the door. There was no time to waste; the baby would be here in nearly 20 weeks! I took the following three days off work to tape and paint in preparation for "Operation Mural" later that weekend. By Friday morning the nursery was completely green; the mural was traced out and ready to be painted. I'm not an artist, but I am a grinder. I revel in the smallest of details, striving for perfection. If people didn't see my work, in this case my mural, as nothing short of amazing, I was gutted. Equally important to me was pace. Since I was a child, I worked at one speed and one speed only: 299,792,458 meters per second.

By the time I returned to work on Monday morning, the nursery was nearly complete. On the wall, near the window, I had painted a large light brown tree bent by an imaginary wind. Leaves scattered across the wall, fluttering lightly in the same breeze. Hanging from a low branch was a little pink monkey leaning over to keep a watchful eye on Abby. Of course I didn't call it pink to Ellen, instead I described as "Dawn's Reveal," remembering the name from the paint swatch. I also wall mounted a tapestry which we purchased while on the floating islands of Uros in Peru several years prior. It hung on a branch that I collected from the front yard that weekend and painted creamy white. As a final touch, I painted one of the Peruvian style birds from the tapestry sailing on that same faux breeze blowing in from the closed window. Nursery phase one complete, and it felt like my first real contribution to the pregnancy since conception.

Ellen entered the room with a big smile. "Wow baby, that's really amazing. Gosh, I hope they're right about us having a girl."

WEEK 21:

GHOST OF
CHILDBIRTH FUTURE

One afternoon, Ellen approached me with some research she had done regarding birthing classes. Ellen loved research. I had always suspected Ellen would be the type to want to attend birthing classes, and I was fine with that. As a matter of fact, I looked forward to it. If television had taught me anything, it was that the sexiest part of pregnancy was the birthing class.

Birthing classes conjured up images of attractive young couples sitting in semi-circles in a large open room with hardwood floors on thin rubber mats. Each "mom to be" decked out in full maternity yoga gear in variations of light pinks, purples, greens and yellows. Some of them were even depicted with their younger, less pregnant little sisters. They'd talk about the experience of being pregnant. They'd smile cheerfully, clutching their soft pillows while describing the deep longing they felt to get back to working out. Others would discuss how much they missed dancing and how they would eventually return full time to the independent dance studio in the heights. We would cover important subjects like daily affirmation and the importance of sitting behind our wives while cupping their bellies with our open palms, for reasons I hadn't yet learned.

That Saturday morning, instead of eating delicious vanilla cinnamon French toast at home, we made our way to the birthing "school." As we wound through nearby neighborhoods, Ellen assured me she knew the way.

"Turn right here, right at the next road and then you'll follow it to her house, which should be on our right."

House? I wasn't against the classes being in a house, but if my studio dreams were going to be fulfilled, this house should look more like a New York loft than a suburban split level. As we pull up to the driveway, I saw several SUV's littered with the all-too-common A&M or, conversely, UT college stickers in the rear window.

We walked up to the front door and saw a blurred figure across the room waving us in through the beady glass windows of the main entry. We slowly pulled the door open and peeked around the corner like terrified teenagers in an 80's horror flick looking into an abandoned log cabin.

Once inside, we saw a cramped living room with several other uncomfortable-looking couples twisting around to watch us enter. They were sitting with their backs to us and I sensed that we had just broken a very awkward silence. The men's eyes screamed "Run!" while the women's eyes screamed "Shhhhhh." The fear resonating from the men's fluttering chests was palpable, while the woman appeared to be under some sort of spell, drunk in anticipation of answers to questions men could never comprehend.

As my eyes moved towards the center of everyone's attention, I sensed the subtlest of movement. I slowed for a moment, like a startled antelope that just smelled the lion that had been stalking it across the savanna. My whole body tensed, that feeling you get when you don't know exactly what's going on, but you know it's bad. You just freeze in a kind-of "what the hell is happening!?" moment.

Camouflaged perfectly in the corner against floral printed wallpaper was a chair with similar upholstery. The chair gradually appeared like some twisted stereogram you needed to stare at for several moments to reveal the hidden image. Within that chair was a woman. She, too, was masked in the clever disguise of a floral blouse. The whole arrangement was like Wonder Woman's jet, just outlines of shapes all blending together under the same spotty wall behind them. If you squinted, she almost looked like a single floating severed blond head and two pale hands waving us forward. It was eerie, and in my mind she would forever be the ghost of childbirth past, present and future.

The floating head was named Beverly and it greeted us with a big smile, like the Cheshire Cat materializing in the air before us. With a single swooping hand, she commanded us to pick a seat from any of the unmatched chairs and loveseats in the room before us. It's a trap! My head swung around to evaluate where the exits of the room were, relative to our location. Ellen smiled and arbitrarily picked the velvet loveseat directly before Beverly, despite my efforts to pull her in the direction of the much less conspicuous chairs against the wall.

As usual, Ellen picked the least practical seat in the room, the seat in the front of the room: the teacher's pet seat. The only seat that left us vulnerable to attacks from behind, with no clear view of the exit. The seat Ellen chose was back on to everyone, except one other couple directly across from us on the opposite wall next to Beverly. This left me with two choices, stare at Beverly's floating head, or consistently get caught awkwardly staring at the couple opposite us. Perfect!

The couples in the class smiled. The men smiled nervously. And no one in the room was introduced. The daddies wanted to be polite, I could tell, but there was no time for pleasantries; they were shutting down. I wasn't the only one struggling with the family room format. After several minutes of awkward silence, the last couple walked in. They too were greeted by the same hypnotic movements from Beverly. They sat down in the last remaining location, the seats that I would have chosen. This prompted Beverly to perk up like a robot whose motion detector had just been triggered. She didn't speak, she just sat forward and put her hands together. She stared blankly at the back of the room for what seemed like minutes. The women appeared to lean towards her like plants in the warm sun. The men: well, I shouldn't speak for the rest of the men, but I was bewildered.

Most of the couples in the room seemed relatively normal, not normal to my "New York Loft Yoga Mat Fantasy," but normal enough for the south. The couples were at various stages of pregnancy from "I could pass as cute but chubby" to "if I move too quickly, I'll have this baby right now." One girl was strictly limited to behavior mimicking that of a possum. She couldn't do normal things like standing or reacting. If I threw a Frisbee at her head, she would be left with two choices: take a Frisbee in the face or have a baby. If I were in that position, the last thing I would want to do was drive half way across town to be told how fragile our pregnancy might be. I couldn't live with that kind of uncertainty, but apparently she was fine with it.

I rationalized her ability to cope with my OBGYN theory. Young girls visited OBGYN from puberty on, and each visit ended with them simply being told that their vagina remained intact. They had no reason to be afraid of the doctor. By the time they hit their twenties, they were already numb to all the sights, sounds, smells and procedures of a doctor's office. Men, on the other hand, only went to the doctor when something was wrong. There was never good news at the doctor for us, only problems. This was the only logical explanation as to why the pregnant possum didn't live in fear of getting hit with a Frisbee. Instead, she leaned back in Beverly's raggedy old rocking chair and relaxed. If anything, she seemed to find comfort in pregnancy and all the horrors that accompanied it. Her husband's demeanor further supported my theory. Either he had just spent thirteen weeks on a desert island without sunscreen or he was on the verge of stroking out.

It always amazed me what people found comforting. Two years before at Christmas, my wife and I traveled to the Texas Hill Country to spend time with her family. Her side of the family is awesome. I loved them like blood from the moment I met them. Whenever we are together, we have a great time. Ellen's mom's birthday was on Christmas Eve and we were going to go to her mother's Lutheran church. Usually, I wasn't a church fan, but recently Ellen and I had begun going to the Greek Orthodox

Church. If you've ever been, it's like watching a *Lord of the Rings* film, in Greek, except without subtitles and the cool visuals. It is two and a half hours of indecipherable chanting with a 5 minute English sermon as an intermission. So, the notion of a one hour English sermon, where jeans are permitted, may as well have been Santa's Village.

Normally, in church, I struggle to focus on one of two things. The first: not cursing loudly and without reason while people worshiped in silence. I never had this fear, until my wife fool heartedly asked me one day if I had ever worried about shouting profanity in church. Thanks, Baby. The second was sex.

We pull up to the church and it looked like any other little Hill Country church: small, but quaint. Except tonight, it looked beautiful beyond its own humble bones as it had been blanketed with a thin layer of snow. 'The perfect Christmas Eve', I thought. As we walked inside, the theme was consistent. There were a modest number of pews occupied by modest Texas hill country folk. As we sat down, a strikingly attractive family in the forward most pew caught my attention. As the service began, I remained focused on the mom's long blonde hair draping over the back of her pew. As usual, I began my construction of her sex life 'Hmmm, young with two kids. Maybe she was a virgin when she met her husband. Sure, she's only been with one man physically, but while he's at work and the kids are in day care, she would watch porn and fantasize about orgies and sex with women.'

About thirty minutes into my fantasy, out of nowhere, she stood up and walked to the front of the church. 'Oh shit, it happened!' I thought in a panic 'She heard my thoughts. No!!

Even worse, God told her what I was thinking!!!' She sat beside the podium and grabbed a nearby guitar. She stared out into the congregation and smiled; her eyes grew wide, but not in a good way. This was a creepy, exaggerated, 1950's classic cartoon kind of scenario. She immediately seemed ethereal and slow, like she was moving underwater. She tuned her guitar, still grinning to the point that it looked painful.

Once satisfied that she could channel the profound joy she felt from the instrument, her head clicked backwards. She rooted her manic gaze on the parish. Her jaw nearly trembled with a bliss fueled by a thousand suns. Delicately, she strummed her well-manicured nails across the strings. The children of the church moved forward though the aisle, like sailors steered towards the rocky coastline, drawn in by the songs of a deadly siren. Between strumming the guitar and praising God's glory, she wiggled her finger at the children's noses as she sang. By the time she had finished, I was completely numb from the vision of this glee-riddled zombie. Her purity was terrifying to me, yet somehow everyone else in the room found it warm and inviting.

Beverly was less like a church siren and more like a hormone harpy. She was a dog whistle for the pregnant, while the men in the room heard nothing. When her silence finally was broken, it was to commend us for taking on a post-conception education. She went on to describe some of the topics we would be covering in class. What to expect in pregnancy, labor and delivery, drugs, medical interventions, cord blood, circumcision, recovery, vaccination and swaddling, to name a few. She also noted that class would run about three hours and followed no particular format. Three hours?! Maybe

I could duck out unnoticed and catch a Greek Orthodox Church service just to break things up a little. She went on to explain that there would be six classes, totaling eighteen hours. Sigh.

PIT THE SHIT
OUT OF HER

Only 18 weeks left. I needed to finish the nursery. Baby Abby was sprinting towards us, her wobbling little silhouette on the horizon. I wanted to start on my most ambitious project yet: trying to one-up the image of the curtain rod made from a branch that I found on the internet while brainstorming nursery ideas. Since seeing that Google thumbnail, every tree I saw was little more than a really crappy curtain rod auditioning for Abby's nursery.

Was my quest for the perfect curtain rod random and excessive? Yes, but I wanted Abby's nursery to be exceptional. Working on the nursery was therapeutic for me. It made the pregnancy tangible. Not to mention Ellen left me alone, so for once I was actually allowed to make a decision on something baby related.

Initially, crape myrtles interested me; foreign to my native island of Newfoundland, they were exotic. I was amazed by the strange bark-less trees with flowers that bloomed in shades of white, pink, purple and everything in between. One crape myrtle in particular got my attention. The tree could be seen from the office window of one of my employees, a naval architect named Danny. Daily, whenever I walked into his office, I was distracted by the perfect curtain rod waving at me in the wind just beyond the glass.

After several weeks of obsessing, I developed a plan. Cameras protected the parking garage and main entrances to the building, but there was a road just behind the tree on the other side of the fence beyond the property line. I could come to work early and sneak out the emergency exit of our office. It led to the courtyard where the tree awaited; I could cut the limb and lob it over the fence. Re-entering the building through the door was easy, as long as I rigged it not to lock behind me, at which point I was free to leave through the parking garage and drive to the nearby road to pick it up.

Over the next several mornings, I performed a stake-out near the drop location and it became obvious to me that the operation would be threatened. An ant trail of large dogs walked by old men decked out in bright orange vests and blinking lights lined the streets from 4am forward. The curtain rod would need to be extracted by some other route. Spotting me in the bushes before dawn with a hand saw would have undoubtedly been just the kind of thing to send these old men into a geriatric frenzy. They'd be dialing 911 on their *Jitter-Bug* cell phones faster that I could say *"Absorbene Jr."* I needed a better plan.

That plan came to me, later that week, while circling the parking garage on my way home. There was another way to extract the branch. In a non-parking corner of the garage, by a small mechanical room, there was a tiny path. A quick hike confirmed my suspicion, the maintenance guys must have used it as a short cut to access the building's AC units, which were luckily located near my curtain rod. It was perfect, the only thing in my way was a small waist high chain link fence with a locked gate.

The next morning I told Ellen my plans, not because I thought she'd approve, but because I thought she may question why, at 4am, I was completely dressed in my black Ninja paintball gear. It was still dark when I arrived at the office, and it would stay that way for at least two more hours. Once parked, I unloaded my black duffel bag of equipment, which included a measuring tape, a saw and a limb cutter. I slung it over my shoulder and headed towards Checkpoint Bravo, AKA the tree, AKA Abby's curtain rod. As I approached the tree, even in near complete darkness, the seemingly perfect branch appeared to lean in a direction not visible from the perspective of the office window. I had been duped, like the red lights of a strip club turned a meth-head into a starlet. I now saw the twisted, mangled reality of the branch up close and personal.

I knelt under branch to see if there was any way it could be salvaged. Not only was it bent, it was too tall, like twenty feet too tall. If it were to fall toward the road it would either hit a power line or flip over the fence swatting the blinking, vested old men like fireflies. The other options were no better. If it were to fall towards the building, at a minimum I would break one of the windows. If it were to fall away from me, it would hit the AC units. The only other option, and discouragingly, the best option, would be for it to fall towards me. This would have most likely resulted in me being skewered by a twenty foot long crape myrtle branch. Danny would likely show up for work several hours later, looking out his window to find an impaled ninja lying in the mulch.

This tree had just robbed me of two hours sleep. I looked up at the tree and wished that a hurricane would tear it from the ground and toss it into the road like a juggling pin. Maybe an AC unit would catch fire early enough in the morning that the tree would slowly burn to death while the old men were sleeping. Defeated, I walked back down the narrow footpath, got into my truck and returned home to get changed for work. Predictably, Ellen found more humor in the story of my failed attempt to extract the curtain rod than any deliberate joke I'd made since marriage. Nursery phase two aborted.

"The doctors used to say *pit the shit out of her*," Beverly said in response to my wife's inquiry into the appropriate application of Pitocin.

The first half of our second birthing class was going to be a question and answer period for the women regarding various aspects of pregnancy and delivery.

"They do it to speed up labor. They don't care whether you need an epidural. They want to make it to the golf course by tee-time," she continued.

The women recoiled while the men in the room slumped forward, predicting the rest of their weekend would be spent listening to emotionally charged conversations revolving around the "P-word." Beverly spent the next two hours answering Pitocin-related questions in ways that resolved nothing for the young mothers in the room.

"Why?"

"How can they do that?"

"Don't doctors take a code of ethics?"

The final segment in our Saturday Morning Fun Fest would be the meditation session. But this wasn't the legitimate type of meditation you'd expect to find in a Tibetan Monastery. This was basically an absurd exercise, much like nap time, except instead of children in a day care it was a bunch of strangers in Beverly's living room spooning to the sounds of the ocean. As ridiculous as it was, anything was better than the questions. The canister of Pitocin tear gas Beverly had lobbed into the room earlier that Saturday morning left a thick cloud of anxiety hovering in the air, so lying on the floor was probably our best option.

Beverly took her time, explaining how to lie down.

"Let's begin. First, our feet should be placed firmly on the floor."

Why did this need explanation? Did someone at some point actually stand up on the chair, disrobe and take a swan dive into the beige berber carpet below?

"Then, slowly kneel down rotating the hips, lying on your left side," she continued.

This was to dissuade anyone from crumbling to the floor from a standing position like the collapsing toy figures I played with as a child.

"Now, Men, you do the same, spooning *behind* your partners."

One could only assume this was aimed at deterring the more delicate men in the room from taking the forward-most spooning position, in front of their partners. Forget the inherent risk that someone might confusedly spoon one of the complete strangers in the room.

After carefully following her complicated instructions on how to lie down, I glanced around the room looking for anything interesting to stare at. I found pictures of Beverly and her family at various ages over the years as they travelled the country. I looked at her mismatched decor, her unsettling cherub collection and her dog, barely visible under the baby gate leading to the kitchen. But the only thing in the room that held my attention was a set of nicely pedicured feet. I liked feet, not in a creepy Quentin Tarantino "I must have a nude foot close up in every film" kind of way, but in an "I would be okay with touching those feet" way. I felt like nice feet were a good indication of the rest of the woman's body. Pampered, soft feet probably meant that they cared about all of the bits and pieces of their body not usually displayed in public. I was surprised by how nice pregnant feet could look. I had the impression that, once the pregnancy began to show, the feet and ankles turned into swollen blotchy hoof-like things. Maybe that came later.

"Okay. That's it for this week. Try practicing this at home," Beverly directed, after the forty something minutes of nothing was over.

"How did that feel for everyone? It's paramount that you all remain focused on your breathing, and I could tell that everyone was very much in the moment. Well done."

"Great," I replied.

Leading up to our next doctor's visit, Ellen began discussing her visions of childbirth with me more frequently. Discussions on topics I had thought we'd aligned on long before getting pregnant. Not surprisingly, after the "pit the shit out of her" comment at our last birthing class, Ellen dove deeper into her research regarding childbirth and medical interventions.

What alarmed me was the subtle use of key words. These were codes that came up more and more frequently as the weeks went on, words like "natural", as in "How could one ensure that the birth would be natural"; or "intervention", as in "How can one avoid unnecessary interventions?" I sensed that our OBGYN was being sabotaged by Beverly and that her position was being reinforced by emotive books provided by friends that were privy to our secret. In the evenings that led up to our next doctor's appointment, it wasn't uncommon to be disrupted from my sleep at 3am to find Ellen pawing at the air.

"No... Pitocin... nooooo..." or "D-o-o-o-o-n't epidural... d-o-o-o-o-n't."

I sensed any previous deals we'd made regarding midwives were probably off.

ABBY VS. THE CHICKEN SANDWICH

I t was late, and as we drove to the emergency room, Ellen, breathing deeply, explained that during the day she had stopped for a meal after shopping. Against her own advice, she decided on a fried chicken-sandwich. Ellen had carefully avoided fast food until now, trying to meticulously control whatever she put in her mouth. Ironically enough, she was only weeks away from losing complete control of every word that came out of it. But it had been a long day, and she knew that trying to make it home while Abby was hungry just wasn't going to happen.

Some women had cravings for pickles and ice cream, and my wife did too, but mostly she craved protein, and when she was hungry it was paralyzing. Fortunately for Ellen, directly next to the shopping center was what she believed to be a reasonably healthy fast food alternative.

Sleeping that evening, on my coma-inducing memory foam pillow, I woke up to the pained sounds of violent food poisoning. Ellen was in trouble and I knew it. This wasn't the "my belly hurts" type of food poisoning, this was the "once in a decade" type food poisoning, and her body was weak from the pregnancy. Normally, she was an impenetrable gastronomical fortress. Just a few years prior, we had spent Christmas in Peru hiking the Inca Trail, and of the eleven people present, she was one of the few whose belly remained unscathed. From that time onward, I was convinced that somewhere in her DNA laid the key to unlocking salmonella resistant chickens. Not anymore.

The minutes passed like hours as I listened through the wafer-thin door of our bathroom and waited for a break in her illness. I expected to hear a deep sobbing cry ring out at any moment. Afraid she might open the door buckled over in pain with tears rolling down her weeping face as she clutched a blood soaked nightgown, I was powerless. Anxiously, I waited for her sickness to subside long enough that I could be heard, "Baby, it's time to go to the ER." My gut told me it was already too late: how could Abby defend herself in such a toxic environment?

We arrived at the hospital around 2am. Thankfully the lobby was nearly empty and we were immediately admitted. The nurse led us to a large double room with a single bed; I helped Ellen up and took a seat directly next to her. It was quiet except for a small TV mounted in the corner tuned to static with the volume turned down. I stared at the scrambled grey lines, and all I saw was the black and white images from our last ultrasound. It felt like it took forever for the tall lady in blue scrubs to walk into our room. She didn't introduce herself: she just went directly to Ellen. I immediately began to explain the situation while she searched for a vein in my wife's arm.

"Let me check her blood. As long as that looks fine and she isn't running a fever, the baby should be okay," she said as she walked away having filled the small vial with blood.

"Thank you, nurse," I said politely.

She slowed to a stop in the doorway.

"I'm not a nurse," she said, firmly looking back over her shoulder.

"Sorry, doctor," I replied nervously, understanding that being called a nurse in her eyes was probably only a single pay grade away from being called a garbage man.

Exhausted, Ellen slowly rolled her head toward me and whispered, "Baby, I think she's a nurse practitioner."

What the hell?! That's what I called her when she stopped in the doorway like an insulted cowboy in a spaghetti western. Meanwhile, our unborn child was shaking like a leaf inside my wife's poisoned uterus. Ellen, always ready to explain the mysteries of the world, took a moment from her illness to fill me in. Somewhere between a nurse and a doctor there was a medical missing link called a Nurse Practitioner. It didn't matter to me; I decided they were merely overly educated, overly sensitive nurses.

We waited nearly an hour for the results to come back. Ellen slept as I sat on the uncomfortable hospital chair, bouncing my leg frantically like *Def Leppard's* one-armed drummer. I was anxious. Waiting for test results, particularly blood tests, wasn't something I was particularly good at. To someone less interested in my personal history, this could be tossed into the "hypochondriac basket," but there was more to it than that.

Early in our relationship, Ellen and I had both agreed to get tested for STD's. I was excited by this: nothing put a spring in my step more than the promise of unprotected sex with a hot twenty-three year old. I virtually skipped to the doctor's office that Monday to get checked out. My doctor was a young Asian man who spoke broken English, and what he lacked in bedside manner, which was vast, he made up for in talent. So I tolerated him. Every nostril, ear and eye would be inspected with intensity, like some cloudy pool of water that masked a giant cancer-filled sea monster, dwelling below. At some point during most any visit, he placed his finger against his lip and stared back at me, furrow-browed for minutes, only to announce that I would somehow survive my sinus infection, if I took ALL of the antibiotics he prescribed.

This time, he quickly drew blood and explained that I would get a letter by Wednesday of next week as long as everything was fine. Otherwise, I would get a call to come in to the office and discuss my results. This was same weekend Ellen was acting in a local production of *Extremities*, and I already had tickets for that Friday night. I was going to be sitting front and center with a small group of Ellen's friends, whom I would be meeting for the first time. I couldn't wait to see her, and I could only assume that being introduced to her friends was a sign that she had thought that I was a keeper.

Every day after work, I rushed to the apartment complex's mailboxes, only to find glossy sixty percent off coupons for custom framing. Wednesday came and went, but I wasn't worried, knowing that I was fine. The Friday of the big show, I arrived home from work and ritualistically hit the mailboxes. Again, there were no test results. I didn't care. It was just a loose end, and one way or the other it was going to be a great night of theatre. Walking into my apartment, laying my bag by the door, I noticed the answering machine blinking on the far wall. I hesitantly walked over, hit the play button and listened.

"Mister James, it's Doctor Kim. Call me about test results, we must discuss."

I snatched the phone off its base and scrambled to my bedroom as I dialed the doctor's office, "Hi, this is James Vavasour. I'm calling about my AIDS test."

The administrator calmly responded, "The doctor is busy now. Can I have him call you back?"

"No, I just wanted to make sure the results from my AIDS test are negative. Can you, at least, please tell me that?" I pleaded.

"I'm sorry, Doctor Kim wants to discuss the results with you directly. He'll call you when he's free." Click.

I walked into my AIDS-filled bedroom, sat on my AIDS bed and called my father, fearing I was dangerously close to blacking out. He didn't answer, so I left him a quick message letting him know that in all likelihood I would be dead before he returned my call. I hung up, laid back on my deathbed and imagined how I would tell Ellen that I had contracted AIDS.

After twenty long minutes, and eighteen fabricated death scenarios, I was startled by the ringing of the phone I had been gripping tightly in my fist the entire time. My thumb already in position, I gently forced the flashing amber talk button down. "Hello?"

"Mister James, Doctor Kim, I never had chance to send letter, test results fine."

Though I had a brutally stressful afternoon, I still enjoyed my evening. Watching Ellen on stage was incredible, and I was deeply impressed by her performance. That evening, we spent our first night together, along with her best friend, stranded in my SUV on the flooded I-10 freeway in tropical storm Allison.

Nearly ten years later, my dramatic actress was still by my side. Our play unfolding as I prayed that Ellen's blood test results would be fine. When I wasn't praying, I was thinking of the sad couple at the anatomy ultrasound and watching Ellen sleep soundly on the hospital bed. It was sometime around noon when a young nurse walked in with crackers and a can of *Sprite*. She was a good nurse, the kind who smiled regardless of how long her shift may have been and how tired she must have felt.

"I have some snacks for you; *Sprite* has no caffeine, so it won't hurt the baby," she said as she laid them down next to me with a small Styrofoam cup and a bendy straw.

'Ellen will be pleased,' I thought, having gone on several bendy straw scavenger hunts for her in our nine years together. No matter how sick she'd gotten, there was something about a bendy straw that always made her feel better.

"Let's wake her up," said the nurse. "I want to take her temperature." Ellen sat forward and began sipping from the small cup of *Sprite*. "Yeah, she's fine," the nurse said calmly with a big smile. "The blood tests should be back soon. If you guys need anything just let me know, I'll be around the corner."

The nurse practitioner returned to the room several cups of *Sprite* later. This time she was smiling: the test results indicated the baby was fine. Ellen's blood was clean, the pleasant nurse was right. Abby was intact. Time to update the "obvious" list of things to avoid while pregnant: alcohol, sushi, roller-derby, poison, and fried chicken sandwiches.

WEEK 24:

THE EVIL
BUTCHER

"James, I've read three books. At this point, you just need to trust me. There is never a good reason for an epidural."

"But say, for example, the doctor, for whatever reason, approaches me with the choice between the health of the baby and an epidural?" I said unequipped with the knowledge I needed to win the argument at the time.

"No," she replied. "That doesn't make any sense."

As the conversation went on, I began to regret that we had made the decision to have children so soon. Clearly, I needed more time. I just couldn't keep up with the frantic pace my wife had set. Somehow, she had squeezed seven years of medical school into the first five months of pregnancy. At times, I found it difficult to decipher if her knowledge was rooted in medical fact or just hyperbole generated from zealous books and opinionated friends. Sometimes, I assumed it was simply stubbornness. She came from a long line of stubborn, or self-proclaimed "strong women" and Ellen carried on her mother's tradition well.

Early in our relationship, I recognized her mother's stubbornness through a dog. I knocked on the front door to Ellen's mom's impressive house. By Texas standards, it was a middle class home. By my standards, it was the Taj Mahal. I knocked as politely as I could, and was quickly greeted by a beautiful middle aged lady. Nice, I thought to myself, that's probably what Ellen's going to look like at that age. Smiling, thumbs in my pocket, nervously tapping my fingers against my thighs, I noticed that she was struggling. Something very large was pushing against her behind the half open door, and it appeared to be a dog.

"Come on in," she said. "Don't mind Sampson, he's friendly. Ellen's upstairs getting ready; she'll be down in a minute."

"Thank you," I replied, trying my best to hide that I was already fantasizing about her daughter's naked body glistening under the steamy hot water of the shower.

Sampson was friendly. He was a golden retriever, except he was red and looked more like an Irish Setter that had swallowed a Golden Retriever. He was huge, with a foaming muzzle that looked like he just took first prize in a rabid bat eating contest. As soon as I cleared the entry way, Sampson stuffed his frothy mixture of snot, drool and dirt into my crotch. "Hey, buddy!" I winced as I pushed his Dodge Omni sized head away. I tried to slip past him to follow Ellen's mom into the living room.

"I'm Karen," Ellen's mom said. "I'm guessing you are James. Ellen has told me a lot about you."

I followed her into the living room while Sampson buried his frothy snout in my ass. By the time Ellen finally made her way down, it looked like I had rode to her house straddling a Clydesdale on a saddle made from slug hides.

As we continued dating, Ellen learned that I wasn't a filthy man with naturally foaming genitals, but a victim of Samson's gentle heart. On each new date, Ellen's mother saw me strategically twisting and turning past Sampson like a college quarterback. I even resorted to bribing him with large husks of rawhide, but Sampson swallowed them like pills, and quickly returned to the only thing he hadn't been able to finish: my groin. In my obvious frustration, it wasn't long before Karen labeled me as a dog hater.

"James, is Sampson bothering you? I know you don't like dogs," Karen would say.

One evening, we were all sitting down to eat dinner. Sampson, as usual, was grinding his cappuccino-like snout between my legs, while Ellen insensitively laughed across the table from me. Karen walked inside from the backyard. She carried perfectly grilled T-Bones that she had just finished a few moments earlier. As she reached down to place the steak on my plate, Sampson perked up and tried to intercept. In the heat of the moment, I tapped the top of his snout with my index finger and firmly said "No."

Karen was furious. In a single swat of Sampson's nose, she saw custody battles, restraining orders and a single mom raising an emotionally and physically scarred grandchild.

"DON'T HIT MY DOG!" Karen threatened loudly.

"He was about to get my steak. I just tapped him with my finger. He didn't even feel it."

She got up and walked into the kitchen, reached into a drawer and pulled out what thankfully wasn't a 9mm handgun. Instead, she had a bright white and green spray bottle. Briskly, she returned to the table, standing above Sampson and me.

"Don't hit my dog. SAMPSON DOWN!"

With that, she pointed the spray bottle and maced Sampson in his developmentally challenged face. Sampson slowly recoiled, like a moray eel, beneath the kitchen table. She laid the bottle in front of me.

"If he jumps up, spray him with this. Do not hit him again."

Sampson walked away to the safety of the living room while I turned the bottle around to read the bright green front label: *Bitter Apple*. I'd never seen dog mace before. I spun the bottle around, hoping to read the ingredients when large bold black text caught my attention.

Caution: Avoid spraying in eyes.

"Karen, I don't think you are supposed to spray this in the dog's eyes. It even says so here. I think this is meant for furniture, to stop them from chewing."

"That's not how I use it." Karen explained her position with great clarity.

"You think that might be why his face is always covered in thick white foam?" I asked rhetorically.

Years passed and Sampson moved on to the great big crotch in the sky. Yet somehow, my title of Dog Hater remained firmly intact. Ellen and I were married and we eventually decided it was time to try our hand at parenthood. We bought a small white Malti-Poo named Notorious P.Y.G., Pygmy for short. She was our newly adopted baby. Pygmy quickly grew to be my kindred spirit in puppy form. I would have thrown myself in front of any car in the city to protect her. I even made shirts and mugs with her likeness, blinged out with a platinum grill, pimpin' chains and iced out earrings, mostly to torment Ellen.

None of this changed Karen's mind about my lack of affinity for dogs. When we moved into our first home and Karen came to visit for the weekend. I found her graciously cooking in the kitchen with Ellen.

"Hey ladies!" I said, lying down on the floor next to Pygmy just before giving her a belly zerbert.

Her mom gazed in disbelief.

"You don't think its gross kissing her belly like that? You don't like dogs... she's a dog?!" she announced, as if I should throw myself back in disgust, not recognizing that Pygmy was, in fact, a dog all along.

This was the same stubborn blood that coursed through Ellen's veins. She had made up her mind. Doctors loathed the act of non-surgical, non-medicated childbirth.

"Ellen, I'm just inclined to believe the doctor. She's the professional. If she decided in the middle of labor that you needed an emergency C-section, epidural or Pitocin, who am I to argue?" I asked.

"Well, I've been doing some research and there's a Hospital that has a Mother's Center with midwives. Maybe they'd be more inclined to try natural interventions," she responded.

I paused, gained my composure, and made sure that I wasn't about to say anything stupid. "Midwives!? Bleh, Midwives are for sellouts! If we really want to have this baby right, all we need is an alleyway. We can deliver her in a dumpster. That is, unless of course, you think the homeless aren't capable of the same things REAL people are?" Ellen shook her head, clearly unprepared to have an intelligent discussion on the matter.

"Ask yourself one question, do you really want some doctor butchering your child's penis?" (Insert the sound of screeching tires here) Beverly began class number three. She spoke with an expression Ellen would describe as her "shit smelling face." My penis and I fell back against the seat in disbelief. We were having a girl, so circumcision wasn't an issue for Abby and Ellen. But this wasn't about babies anymore: this was extremist pro-foreskin propaganda. Attack me, attack my wife, heck you can even attack our unborn child, but DON'T EVER ATTACK MY PENIS! Despite Beverly's accusations, my penis had not been butchered; my penis had been masterfully sculpted by the Michelangelo of pediatricians. His work had been appreciated over the years, and sadly he would never know the joy and wonder his work had inspired; his passion for the perfect penis would probably never be recognized among the medical community. It was about time someone stood up for him and every other circum-scissor-ist. If anything was going to be butchered in this room, it would be *by* my penis. I always thought that naming your penis was stupid, but not anymore. From hence forward, all shall know my penis as "The Butcher."

My childhood memories had indeed included evil Butchers, but they weren't pediatricians, and there were not children being led into salt baths in my tale. I grew up in a couple of places. But the one place I called home and spent my most formative years was Newfoundland, a crazy place filled with magic realism where people not only believe in, but actually fear things like fairies. In Newfoundland, cellars look more like hobbit holes, and nearly every home comes with an ocean view.

When I moved to Newfoundland, the only thing I feared was a group of boys whose last name was "Butcher." It was a five year reign of terror that began in elementary school and continued into junior high. Throughout that time, many appendages were bruised and beaten by the Butchers. My penis wasn't one of them.

I wasn't about to let Beverly be the first. I glanced around the room hoping somehow to unite all the other persecuted penises in the living room, but to my surprise, everyone else seemed completely oblivious.

"You know they don't do this to children in Canada," Beverly proclaimed.

It was too much for me to bear. "I'm Canadian," I said. "I'm circumcised."

"They perform circumcisions on less than 40% of young boys there," she replied to my penis as she squeezed it from the other side of the room like the choking force clutch of Darth Vader.

I felt my wife's tightening grip on my hand. I let go and pushed it aside. I felt her sink in her chair. I raised my hand as I began to speak, "Maybe we should open a clinic, a mutilated penis reconstruction clinic. We could graft new foreskins onto those afflicted by circumcision so they could go on living normal lives. We could even find a smart lawyer to demand money for pain and suffering to help pay for the surgery. I bet we could easily charge 10k per penis, make enough money to live like kings and still fund a sizable circumcision smear campaign." I stopped when Ellen thrust her elbow into my side while whisper-yelling "Enough!"

By our next OBGYN appointment, Ellen had volumes of unanswered questions regarding paralyzing epidurals, pain amplifying Pitocin, vagina splitting episiotomies, and belly busting C-sections.

By the end of the hour-long interrogation, Ellen and I had learned a couple of things. First, doctors, just like me, were good old fashion pessimists that liked to have a Plan A, Plan B and a Plan C. Some might even argue that by initiating Plan C one could save precious time and energy. Secondly, when the decision was made to initiate Plan A, B or C, it wouldn't be by the mother or the father: it would be by the doctor. This decision would be based on any number of factors, including the failing health of the mother, the failing health of the baby, or the doctor's busy schedule that day. Hell, it might even be based on the twins we just found out our doctor happened to be carrying.

WEEK 25:

ABBY "THE BUTCHER" VAVASOUR

llen wasn't the only one doing research. I too had begun my own investigation, summed up into a two word Google search: Pregnancy Sex. I wasn't one of those guys that found pregnancy unattractive. As a matter of fact, with my Google Safe Search set to "Freak" I often found myself paying more attention to the "Image" tab than the "Web" tab. I thought pregnancy was extremely sexy: the glow, the belly; if anything, the "Taboo" may have turned me on even more.

I wasn't alone in this curiosity, clicking the image tab would lead you to images hosted by websites that proclaimed to be "The #1 Pregnancy Sex Site on the Internet!" There were films too, like *Passionate Preggo Sex: 7* for the hopeless romantic. Even stranger were images of pregnancy sex orgies. I only imagined how unnatural those films must have been. The handsome young pharmaceutical salesman walked into the crowded OBGYN's office, cue sleazy music. How did someone find so many pregnant women willing to film themselves having sex with total strangers? There were even entire message boards where bragging husbands could proudly and anonymously post naked images of their wives for the world to see, assuming the world was inclined to perform Google searches for naked pregnant women.

Early in the pregnancy, we continued to have normal sex. I would get a little nervous, but certainly not enough to win an arm-wrestle against my "Over the Top" sex drive. However, as the pregnancy became more visible, a new anxiety began to surface. It was Ellen's belly. The problem was less the belly itself, more the act of lying on or around the belly, even though my research on the internet had provided ample support of the pregnant belly's ability to survive under an orgy of individuals. Somehow, it didn't apply to our pregnancy. In my mind, Ellen's belly wasn't like the bellies found in films like *Passionate Preggo Sex: 7*. It was more like a giant *Zip-Lock* baggie filled beyond capacity with baby, waiting to burst open at a moment's notice. Even worse, the act of sex didn't only involve squeezing the bag, it involved potential contact between the penis and the cervix. In *Zip-Lock* terms, this meant a finger from one hand would fiddle around with the zipper while the other hand tightly clutched down on the bag.

Early on, websites reading: "Sex is safe throughout pregnancy" were definitive green lights to us. Websites reading: "Semen contains natural prostaglandins, which helps ripen the cervix" suggested that, by 40 weeks, we would have a fun and natural strategy to induce labor.

That all changed when Ellen began to show; the first article was dismissed as nonsense. It must have been missing pages or be in reference to couples with a combined weight of less than 180 pounds. While the second article was a revelation, it told me that my penis had been terribly miss-categorized. Clearly it should have been placed in the "alcohol, sushi, roller-derby, poison and fried chicken sandwiches" category a long time ago. My penis may as well have been a flame-thrower launching burning fuel at Abby's front door. And my torso swung around like a huge fleshy demolition ball waiting to collapse her fragile membrane roof.

Sex wasn't an option for me anymore. Answering the question, "How did someone find so many pregnant women willing to film themselves having sex with total strangers?" Simple, Ellen probably wasn't the only frustrated wife left sexless for nearly nine months.

Our fourth birthing class started with a bang. "You find me a sterile vagina, and I'll find you a sterile field," Beverly proclaimed in reference to babies being at risk of infection once a woman's water has broken. Oddly enough, this wasn't the first time I'd associated vaginas with fields.

As a child, Saturday mornings were spent in the local grocery store. Week after week, my mother struggled, knowing that some aisles had to be avoided altogether when I was around—for example, the feminine products aisle. Some advertising genius in the 1970's must have also been thinking of a sterile field when coming up with an advertising campaign for maxi-pads. Even the box itself had a meadow of dandelions decorating the exterior. The notion of a box full of dandelions blowing in the wind thrilled me: I had no real understanding of what was actually in the box, and feminine product commercials in the 1970's gave no indication. There was no "Red Dot" like there is today. There were only fluffy dandelions, playfully being blown by a beautiful woman's profile.

My mother would cringe as we walked past that aisle. My sharp youthful vision would always catch the feminine aisle's clean and colorful floor to ceiling perfection in my peripheral vision. It could only be topped by the sleek lines of a perfectly fronted cereal aisle. I would immediately dart off toward the shelf to pull down a package of maxi-pads. Every time I started to pry those flimsy cardboard flaps open, my mother quickly snatched it away just in time. Sadly, this just fed into my fantasy. Had I been given a chance to open it, I may have gotten a much needed reality check. Instead, I just learned that I would be robbed of any potential fun while shopping with a woman. Crying, I would be pulled away, peering up at the tiny little boxes of dried dandelions.

Beverly used her field analogy to introduce the class to a movie, an "Indie Film" about childbirth. She assured us that the gory images would reinforce the metaphor of a non-sterile field. It was a video from the sixties or seventies, and the hairy meadow of a vagina that leapt all over the screen as Beverly fast forwarded on her VCR was the only connection I made to a field. "Great, the less I'll have to suffer through" I thought as she skipped though the beginning. This was particularly true considering we were again sitting in the velvet grape loveseat, despite my endless complaining about the last couple of classes. Ellen still felt that picking the same seat made sense. In addition to its many shortcomings, today we would experience its neck wrenching view of the television.

"This is a really long video," Beverly said. "So I'll skip straight to active labor."

It wasn't long before I realized that this video was literally a real-time account of this woman's delivery. No editing. No scene selection. No time lapse photography of a baby's head emerging from her mossy overgrown 1970's vagina like a mushroom from the mulch of a decaying forest floor. This would be a three hour marathon of a stranger's unkempt genitalia winking at me while giving birth to a baby I wasn't going to find cute.

The film was as long as it was boring. Beyond an impromptu visit from the woman's priest, there was nothing funny or remotely entertaining about it. Like me, at some point in your life you probably wondered how a young, twenty-something, hormone-raged man, could swear off sex for the rest of his life to fulfill his desire to be a poorly paid priest? Well, here lied the answer. Perhaps his mother shared with him the video of his own birth. Certainly, seminary school wouldn't be such a difficult option anymore. The miracle of childbirth was less like magic and more like "Magic's Biggest Secrets Revealed." Just like the hooded jerk from the 1990's that destroyed every great magic trick ever created, this film killed any mystery there may have been regarding the real function of a woman's vagina. Three hours into the film, my penis' newly instituted nickname "The Butcher" was retired, it was obvious to me who would truly earn that title: Abby "The Butcher" Vavasour.

The past 12 months had felt like the year of the baby. With that came showers, diaper parties and strength in numbers. Most of our closest friends had babies that year, and it seemed each couple had multiple baby showers. One would be thrown for mom by her friends, and another for mom by her colleagues. There was even a baby shower for dad at the office. It didn't end there. The fathers-to-be also had to have a diaper party, a clever plot that must have been developed by diaper companies. What better excuse was there for men to gather for *Ultimate Fighting Championship* pay-per-view events, drink beer and eat burgers than to collect sacks of diapers?

Of course, one guy always brought a pack of *Depends*, but occasionally someone would find new and twisted variation of an actual children's diaper. It was at my own diaper party that I learned of "Denim Diapers." Straight from the mind of pedophiles came the "Daisy Duke" for toddlers. I was already obsessing enough about the imminent midwife threat, I wasn't about to add post-delivery threats like sex offenders into the mix by throwing Abby into a pair of short shorts.

We were fortunate enough to have ridden on the tail end of this long wave of baby making. As a result, we were showered with endless acts of generosity. We were given sacks of used maternity clothes, baby clothes and even larger, more expensive items like car seats, breast pumps, and co-sleepers. These amazing gifts came one after another from friends we trusted. Friends whom, like Ellen and I, spent countless hours researching products that were "Consumer Reports Approved" and "Made in the USA" or, more importantly, not "Made in China."

Not all acts of generosity were as well researched. Oddly enough, thirty year old cribs were one of the more common offerings. Even our middle-aged single male neighbor approached me one day.

"I've got an old crib in the attic if you want it."

I couldn't help but wonder, why the hell this guy would be holding on to a thirty year old crib. Fortunately, these situations were fairly easy to deal with. I would simply say that we had a brand new crib on the way from my father-in-law. Whenever people approached us on the subject of cribs, this was an acceptable answer to keep the questionable attic cribs at bay. The real predicament was rejecting the crib that Ellen's mom, Karen, offered because it was Ellen's childhood crib. It had sentimental value.

"Ellen, don't you want to use your old crib?" Karen asked.

Saying no to this was like saying, go to hell, I reject my childhood and everything it ever stood for! It wasn't that we didn't like the crib, it looked very nice. The problem was that the crib was made of a single header and a single footer with spindles in between making up the bulk of the structure. Not to mention, it has probably been dipped in champagne chip resistant lead paint. The long spindles routed like giant toxic candy canes, positioned perfectly for baby's sore, teething gums. That wasn't the only problem. Spindles are called spindles for a reason, they spin. Sure, a single spindle could offer slow death by way of gradual lead poisoning, but in combination, they became a huge set of baby head gripping Chinese fingers. Ellen herself had fallen. victim to this very crib as a child. We may as well have set Abby down in a bear trap.

Still, the initial and definitive rejection offered by my wife and I wasn't enough to derail the tradition of passing down vintage baby death chambers.

"You used to play in it as a little girl. Remember?" Karen would plead. "You don't want to share that with your children?"

It would even be offered as an antique.

"I know you probably won't use it, but it's over thirty years old, it might be worth something some day? Why don't you just hold on to it?"

Sure, I thought, we'll bury it in our attic deep under a blanket of pink insulation for the next thirty years.

WEEK 26:

THE PERINEALIZER

B y our fifth birthing class, our docile nap time had progressed
to an unfathomable level of humiliation, or perhaps I should
say sex acts, cleverly masked as birthing aids. This was all
some elaborate plan for Beverly to get her voyeuristic freak on, I
was convinced.

"Today, we are going to cover some of the things we need to
do to prepare for the delivery. By 34 weeks, your husband should
start performing nightly perineal massages," she said, staring at
the women of the room.

It always made me uncomfortable when she looked at only
one gender while talking, mostly because that one sex was usually
the women and she used that time to define the husband's newest
"role" in the pregnancy. But as a man, there was one thing worse
than being ignored in a birthing class: being spoken to directly.
Beverly reserved eye contact with the men strictly for issuing

painfully detailed instructions for various humiliating tasks. She continued to explain the benefits of the perineal massage to the ladies, which needed little explanation to me, the concept of stretching the feminine region wasn't new to boys. Even as young pre-pubescent perverts, we had countless jokes about perineal massage under various other names. What I hadn't realized, until now, was that it was more than just a punch line to various juvenile vagina stretching jokes.

Convinced that we now believed a vagina could be "toughened up", Beverly began her demonstration. It was as if she were conducting a miniature orchestra, rolling her two index fingers from side to side rhythmically. She stared at each man, instructing that insertion must be "to the second knuckle." Not until she destroyed every erotic notion I had ever associated with touching a woman's vagina, did she move on. The next category of massage would be the "relaxation massage."

"Oh, it looks like the couple with the blood pressure problem isn't going to make it this week. I hope they didn't deliver yet," Beverly noted, referring to the Frisbee couple.

It felt like they had jumped off a ledge. It almost made me mad, like they threw in the towel. They should still be here, they should be miserable like the rest of us. I looked at Ellen and tried desperately to telepathically communicate the deep and immediate need for her to fake labor so that we could escape like they had. She didn't listen.

"Okay ladies, let's begin. First, our feet should be placed firmly on the floor," Beverly offered, just in case we had somehow forgotten our most recent lesson of how to transition from a seated position to lying on the floor. "Bend at your knees and lay your pillows down in front of you. Now place your chest against the pillow, resting on your elbows while you kneel. Your backside should be up in the air. Dads, kneel down behind your partner and lay your hands on the small of their back."

I looked around the room in my usual astonishment.

"Moms, start rocking from side to side and begin breathing. Dads, tell mom not to stop and that she is doing well."

Was it only me who somehow felt this was just a little inappropriate? I continued to look for any sign of a giggle or sneer.

The men all whispered various inappropriate things, "Yeah… perfect, keep going, that's good, right there."

Watching a room full of people grinding into one another is cool, just not in Beverly's garish living room. Personally, I would have preferred them to not all be pregnant, wearing sweat pants, and certainly not with Beverly prowling the room, nodding in approval.

Ellen looked back at me over her shoulder, fighting back laughter, "You don't have to talk, Baby."

I was grateful that she wasn't onboard either. Massaging Ellen's lower back, I looked around the room and passed judgment on everyone enabling Beverly. I tried to think of something useful that I could sell to these people, not a gimmick like Beverly had sold to us. After all, we had willingly paid for these classes. I tried to think outside the box, what would I be willing to give my hard-earned cash for? What would make this pregnancy easier for me?

Tired of grueling massages to your wife's vulva night after night? Are your index fingers cramped and left aching? Stop being blamed for not fulfilling your husbandly duties! Let Perinealizer do the work for you!

Every night, Perinealizer will sound an alarm to remind your wife to start her massage. It even has a handy ten minute timer. Perinealizer works based on inflate-a-mation technology, sensing and detecting when to inflate to one of its nine inflate-a-mation sizes. It doesn't matter if your wife's vagina is a size one or size four, like Mystic Rains, famous Porn Star and longtime user of the Perinealizer!

"Hi! I'm Mystic Rains. I used Perinealizer every night while training for my new film. When I needed to be a size six for my upcoming movie role, I counted on Perinealizer!"

Call in the next eighteen seconds and get Perinealizer for only six monthly payments of $19.99... But wait, that's not all! Be one of the first 100 callers and you'll get this handy kegel day planner to keep you on track. The phone lines are open! Call now!"

We needed a registry. Ellen and I sat in front of my laptop with lists of "must have" items compiled by friends. We searched each item one by one. The first item on the list was bibs, easy enough. *BabiesRUs.com*, show me your bibs! Within seconds, bibs like "Boys love me", "Heartbreaker" and various other Ed Hardy-looking designs were projected across the screen, the perfect way to raise your own little *Rock of Love* contestant. I tried to search 0-3 month bibs, organic bibs, and anything else I could think of to weed out the slutty ones. Three general categories surfaced, Pink, Blue and Yellow/Green. One might argue that these were in fact colors, and not categories at all. I disagree. When it came to babies, colors stop being colors and start becoming statements, as demonstrated when I innocently moved the mouse over the pink set and clicked "add to registry."

"No!!!" Ellen shouted, like had I just hit the "End Pregnancy" button. "Get the blue ones."

Great, here we go again. "Ellen, there is no pink in the nursery, can we at least buy some pink bibs?"

"Everyone else is going to buy us pink, we need to buy blue."

The internet thing wasn't working for me. Perhaps, if we actually went to the store, things like texture and quality could work themselves into the equation. This might force color into a less dominant position in our decision matrix.

I followed Ellen through the store, leaning over the cart like it was a crutch.

"Oh! We need burp cloths. Which one do you like?" Ellen inquired, so she could take delight in publicly rejecting my recommendation.

"I like the pink and tan set," I replied. Knowing I may as well have said, "Let's find another pregnant woman to have a threesome with us tonight."

"No James, you know that isn't my thing. I'm not into *girl stuff*," she whined.

"Then why do you torment me by continuing to ask for my input. My opinion clearly has no impact on your decision."

"Let's just get the organic green set... do you like those?"

Crippled over the cart, I stared at the huge banners that hung high above us with the cute model babies plastered across them. I thought about the resolution of the image. I wondered what would happen if a baby that big walked into the store. Everyone would freak out. Some would want to hug it and maybe a few would be scared by it. I would probably see it as a threat and preemptively attack it to protect my family. I thought about what people would think if I cracked off one of the stick ponies and threw it across the store like a spear and impaled the giant thrashing mutant in the belly. The image made me laugh, but I also recognized that it probably wouldn't be nearly as funny to me in a few months when all the babies of the world would remind me of my own.

I began comparing the properly scaled babies that were riding around in the strollers and shopping carts with the monster babies on the banner. It surprised me: even the really cute moms had relatively ugly babies in their carts by comparison. I wondered if *Toys R Us* had some sort of genome experiment where they developed different colors of the same perfect baby in a lab. What if our baby looked like me? I looked fine as a man, but I wouldn't have made much of a woman. I'm betting Ellen hadn't thought of that while piling the cart full of sexually ambiguous baby accessories.

"Okay, I think that's it," Ellen looked up at me, "did I miss anything?"

THOSE WHO FAIL TO LEARN FROM HISTORY...

Our final birthing class! I was elated, even though it was yet another video day. This video actually showed promise. Today's film was at least current enough to be in DVD format. Beverly pulled the disk out of the colorful DVD jacket and walked towards the entertainment center. The DVD itself appeared to be professionally manufactured, but the title was impossible to decipher from where I was sitting. Unless some exhibitionistic hippy mom managed to secure a distributor for her bushy vagina gore porn, this would probably not be another dated birthing video.

Beverly pushed the DVD into her VHS/DVD combo player. To my surprise the television displayed a very current, high production value opening title menu that read: *A Blissful Baby*. Beverly gave a quick introduction while I asked Ellen why the DVD looked familiar. By the time Ellen had finished explaining that we actually owned the DVD, and I was supposed to have already watched it, Beverley was ready to start. This was good news indeed. Instead of having to waste valuable personal time to watch some boring baby video, I could kill two birds with one stone in Beverley's living room. Beverly moved to the back of the room and dimmed the living room's yellow glass chandelier for our feature presentation.

The opening sequence began with a reasonably qualified looking mother with early '90's bangs and an ugly blouse holding a crying baby on a bench. She rolled her eyes behind thick glasses while her head flopped back. Clearly she was disappointed with the child that had been delivered to her. She threw her hands up, out of ideas and patience, when a slimy looking man with a stethoscope hung around his neck scooted next to her out of nowhere. He shimmied right up close to her and gave her a creepy, confident nod, like only a man with a Charlie Sheen-worthy rape face could.

He reached into her lap and took the baby, wrapped it up in a blanket like a tiny mummy, and began rattling it over his knee while hissing in its ear. He hissed so loudly and for so long that he turned bright red. A vein surfaced down the center of his forehead so large someone could have hung a wet bath robe from it. Amazingly, the baby went silent. The baby's eyes were expressive in the way that only small dog and small infant's eyes could be, wide and peering up from one side in terror. There it was, "A Blissful Baby", its eyes screaming in silence, paralyzed in fear.

This was yet another example of how someone could get rich in the baby business. The idea was brilliant in its simplicity. Restrain the child, hiss in its ear as loudly as you can and jangle it until its will is broken. Despite the obvious level of success this doctor had accomplished, something about the whole thing just smacked of wrong. It wasn't so much that he essentially tied up the baby, startled the shit out of it, and then shook it into submission. It was more the question of what led him to discover this system.

Like all men, there was no doubt that this was ultimately a scheme to get laid. The quiet baby was merely a vehicle. I theorized that at some point he was just another sleazy guy inspired by the desire to prove that he would be a better father to some hot patient's child than her current husband. He definitely looked the part with his slicked back hair and douchy beard.

Usually, guys like him grazed anywhere that vulnerable women could be found exposing insecurity. You could always spot them roaming around in sleeveless tees at the gym or yoga classes, hoping to find a housewife with a cratering body image. But not this guy, he utilized the perfect combination of both physical and emotional insecurity: postpartum depression. Lay a screaming baby in the woman's lap and even Superwoman would have thrown her arms in the air helpless. This man's baby scare tactics were the Holy Trinity of MILF taming. All he had to do was proudly execute his mastery of subduing their babies and he was in. Frustrated mothers across the country would fall onto their backs, inebriated by the first silence they'd heard in weeks, and whimper, "Now me, doctor, now me…"

When the video ended, Beverly returned to the subject of midwifery, which is a real word. She threw the word midwifery around, deliberately I'm sure, at us at least once an hour. The first time I heard this strange word was about five minutes into the first class and I was mesmerized by it. "Mid-wiff-er-y" I would repeat under my breath over and over. It was fantastically ridiculous. I decided that as soon as I found the time to learn how to sing and play guitar, I would start my soon-to-be world famous glam-rock band. Our name would be Midwifery.

Class was about to end and Beverly was in the midst of her final plea, urging us all to stay in touch. Which, of course, none of us ever would.

"Remember, pregnancy is a natural process and your body is already equipped with everything you need."

Fantastic, at the final minute of the final class, she admits we didn't even need her. It didn't matter, it was over. There was no trophy topped with a polished golden baby head crowning through a vagina, and there was no shiny blue ribbon for the men's penises. Just the joy of being free of Beverly.

Later that afternoon, Ellen informed me that our doubly pregnant OBGYN wasn't going to work for us anymore. This was what the birthing classes had been leading up to, it was meant to butter me up to the idea of midwives. Beverley's repeated pitch was meant to break me in like a greased up baseball glove. Ellen had already set up the appointment, noon on Thursday. We were going to attend a group tour of the Mother's Center. The on again off again subject of midwives had never really been off at all.

We had debated this subject heavily during the "trying" stage. I always felt that a hospital birth with a doctor was the way we would deliver. Ellen believed that being whisked back in time to a large steel tub filled with lukewarm water centered in front of the wood burning fireplace of a civil war era log cabin was the preferred method. We argued endlessly on the matter, but after a ton of failed research, on both purchasing a

DeLorean capable of time travel and securing the location of a civil war era log cabin, we decided a hospital birth was indeed the more practical option. Unfortunately, unbeknownst to me, the archaic practices of the 1800's had slowly crept back into our birth plan.

That Thursday, we went to the Mother's Center to meet the midwives, or as I called them, "the hospital witches." Initially, I found myself pleasantly surprised. Rather than a small cabin with a bear skin rug and a food trough, the Mother's Center was actually a part of a larger practice, with doctors, in the middle of the Texas Medical Center. We made our way to the 18th floor, following another terrified couple that seemed to know the way. Within a few minutes, we had completed registration and were forced into a small room where our midwife, Sunset, was seated in the middle. Surprisingly, she wasn't wearing her hair in a long braid down the center of her back, nor was she wearing frayed dirty white rags like the midwives I had seen portrayed in period films. She was a normal looking woman with scrubs, almost nurse-like.

"I'm glad you guys are investigating the option of using a midwife for your delivery. We believe that childbirth is a natural process, and together, the midwives of this facility have participated in hundreds of successful natural childbirths."

I fought the urge to ask how many unsuccessful natural childbirths they participated in.

Since our last birthing class, I spent considerable time on the notion of Beverly's advocacy that women were naturally equipped for child birth. I wasn't buying it. What do you guess the child mortality rate was 35,000 years ago? Try selling the simplicity of childbirth to a Cro-Magnon woman as she squatted over an ice pan while a herd of woolly mammoths charged towards her. Meanwhile, daddy was off killing reindeer to feed his new girlfriend. I'm guessing earth was one great big prehistoric orgy. Not because cavemen were raised watching the latest porno etched on the wall of some cave, they were simply acting on instinct. They probably needed to impregnate dozens of cave-women just to get an heir to adulthood. Though I was confident in my theory, I figured now wouldn't be the best time to present my case.

Sunset finished explaining what their midwife services had to offer and opened the room for questions. Without hesitation, Ellen's hand shot up. She was enthusiastic, like a pregnant little Nazi saluting. Her allegiance, I could tell, was already sworn to the midwives.

"Can you tell me about Pitocin and epidurals?" she asked.

Sunset was thrilled to comply, she went on to explain in detail the merits of each and why at times they *should* be considered in a natural birth plan. I liked her already. I didn't memorize her explanation word for word, but here's the gist of what every husband should know about Pitocin and epidurals. This will never be explained so clearly again. If natural delivery is not progressing as quickly as it should, an epidural can be used to help the mother relax. Pitocin can be used to stop the bleeding after the baby has been delivered and the placenta is passed. Both could be used in a last ditch effort to avoid a C-Section after all other options have been exhausted; this was especially logical, considering an epidural would be in place once the decision to do a C-section was made anyway. Unfortunately, I had not been equipped with this information six months ago.

I was pleasantly surprised. We were in a hospital, with doctors, Pitocin, epidurals, and heart rate monitors. The midwives even wore scrubs, although the scrubs were purple, which may have manifested some sort of ceremonial significance. The birthing rooms even had showers and Jacuzzi tubs rather than the animal pelts I had anticipated. Maybe Ellen's natural birth plan wasn't going to be as archaic as I had feared.

WEEKS 28 TO 30:

CUT ME

"You're lucky," the medical assistant said at our first midwife appointment. "We don't accept people after twenty eight weeks, you got here just in time." She flipped open her folder, "You'll be meeting Teresa today."

Ellen wasn't the only lucky one in all of this. I would rather deliver Abby myself than have another two-day discussion about Pitocin like we had after leaving each OBGYN appointment. I wouldn't have accepted no for an answer. I would have pulled out a big piece of mercury laced tuna nigiri sushi and held it to Ellen's temple until a midwife agreed to see us.

Teresa tapped on the door and walked inside. She was completely grey, but it was hard to place an age on her. She was thin and healthy, and very attractive for an older lady.

"Okay, so tell me about the pregnancy so far."

Ellen told her about the food poisoning, and our experience with our OBGYN. I sat and observed, carefully watching for any spells or hexes that Teresa may have been applying without Ellen's knowledge. She moved her hand around Ellen's swollen belly and laid what looked like a *Fisher Price* microphone on it. She listened for a moment.

"Okay, everything looks fine!"

She may as well have rattled some bones and chanted to a fertility god, one of which actually hung outside the office door. Where was the ultrasound, blood test, vagina inspection?

"Aren't you going to do an ultrasound?" I asked.

"Nope," Teresa answered in woeful inadequacy.

"Okay, so when will the next ultrasound be?" I asked.

"There won't be, as long as we think everything is going well."

I didn't like how lightly Teresa was taking the whole pregnancy thing. For all we knew, Ellen's stubborn insistence to continue yoga may have tied a loose noose in our baby's umbilical cord. It was probably floating around wildly, as we spoke, waiting for Abby's little head to slip into it. In the prior twenty eight weeks of OBGYN visits, we had accumulated five ultrasounds, several blood tests, and countless urine tests. If for no other reason, I wanted more ultrasound images so I could finish my developing baby flipbook. This casual approach to pregnancy was exactly what I had been afraid of.

It was time to reinitiate phase two of the nursery. I desperately needed something to ground myself in this pregnancy again, something I could control. I couldn't let Abby's curtain rod slip through my fingers like our OBGYN had. The problem with my last failed branch extraction, much like our OBGYN, was that I relied too heavily on a single source. I needed to have a Plan B, Plan C and Plan D in place. This time I would emerge with a better, even more ambitious branch. A vine wrapped crape myrtle. The idea came to me one day while running at Memorial Park when I noticed an amazing vine wrapped branch. It wasn't a crape myrtle and certainly wasn't curtain rod material, but I knew that somewhere in the city hung the perfect vine wrapped crape myrtle curtain rod. All I needed was the time to find it, and with Ellen heading to Dallas for the weekend, I would have plenty. I knew many of the parks around us from running, and one of those parks I remembered as being particularly viney.

The park I believed to offer my best chance at success was named Bear Creek, and it was huge. Buffalo, deer, and presumably even bears lived in this park, kind of huge. Ellen left that Friday, so after work I circled the park and noted the most likely parking places for police. I wasn't keen on being fined for illegal cutting. I searched for corners less frequently occupied by runners, children and buffalo. I mapped out the "Top Ten Places" I might find suitable branches on a hand drawn map. Had the police pulled me over that day, my map may as well have read "Top Ten Places to Commit Rape." This did not dissuade me, I would get Abby her curtain rod. At this point, I am pretty sure she's heard me in utero talking to Ellen about it. She probably also heard Ellen laughing and telling me I was crazy. I thought this would be an important lesson. Daddy might be crazy, but he loved her.

The next morning, I ate a solid breakfast, grabbed my map from the previous day, and before dawn I was already rummaging through the forest. Wondering around the empty park, I kicked and irritated all sorts of sleeping forest creatures, at least those who were sensible enough to still be asleep. I found many branches, but all were unfit for Abby's seven foot long curtain rod. If I had been trying to make canes and walking sticks, I would have already collected enough to equip every artist on *Death Row Records*, but I wasn't.

As the morning progressed, I quickly exhausted most of the locations I'd identified the day before. Things were not looking good. Crawling back into my truck, I headed home. As I rounded the corner, I noticed a small road leading to a part of the park I had never been to: the campground. This was perfect, dozens and dozens of individual little camping lots. Each had a fire pit and a single parking space no farther than five feet away from the tree line. I could easily investigate every site without raising any suspicion.

I pulled into the first unoccupied spot. Wasting no time, I got out of the car, walked past the barbeque pit and headed into the woods. It was still early, nearing dawn, and I could hear all the little forest creatures stirring as their biological alarm clocks told them morning was on the way. Working my way deeper into the woods, I noticed what looked like a small clearing ahead. This is it, I thought pushing through the tall grass.

There was something unsettling about being knee deep in venomous animal bedding. Slowly moving forward, gently laying one foot in front of the other, I continued. Nearly one third of the way to the clearing, the grass erupted into a chaos of grunts and movement. A heavy and very distressed mammal bolted away from me. Dangerously close to fainting and urinating, I looked to the clearing expecting to see a wild boar launch into visibility. It didn't. This was the worst case scenario. Worried it was some sort of elaborate hillbilly trap, I cracked off a nearby limb and held it like a baseball bat and pushed forward.

I made it safely to the clearing, having survived without any form of ambush. I spotted a huge tree on the far side that I had mistaken earlier for several smaller trees. It was the biggest crape myrtle I'd ever seen, and it was completely swallowed by vines. This was too good to be true.

It was light now, and I could safely navigate the knotted, tentacle-like base of the tree without cracking my neck. I made my way closer and searched from branch to branch of the tree's dense canopy, hoping to spot Abby's curtain rod, and eventually I did.

The perfect vine wrapped branch revealed itself to me, hanging directly above my shoulder, moving in the wind as if waving to me. I almost felt the tree lean forward, like it intended to extend its beautiful arm, sighing with relief that its destiny had finally been fulfilled. It may have been the breeze, but I'm sure I heard a deep guttural moan.

"I've been waiting for you James," the tree seductively whispered. "Cut me."

Nursery phase two complete.

WEEK 31:

ARE YOU SURE IT'S A GIRL?

had been waiting a long time for this day to come, the day we would get to have our 3D Ultrasound of Abby. Finally, I could see if she looked like me, like Ellen, like a combination of us both, or like Sloth from *The Goonies*. Initially, we would have had our OBGYN do this for us, but she was busy having twins. It involved a computer so the midwives were obviously out, we needed to investigate other options. Not surprisingly, again someone decided to cash in on the business of babies, and as always we were there to lap it up. There were several services available in town established exclusively to perform 3D ultrasounds, the one we chose was called "The Whole Story."

We walked into the lobby to find a waiting room that looked a lot like a gift shop. Mugs, T-shirts and photo packages were all available, custom made with your baby's digitized orange face plastered across them. We checked in, pretending it was any other doctors' office, and took a seat. We tried to settle on one of the 3D ultrasound packages offered. We wanted one that was frugal enough that we weren't wasting money on junk we didn't need, while at the same time, not leaving the impression we were disappointed or somehow thought our rendered baby image was ugly. The various options were clearly identified on a large laminated construction paper poster against the far wall. It claimed "Package A" was the best deal, with a CD of pictures, color DVD video and printed color images for $99. By color, I assumed they meant orange like every other 3D ultrasound I had ever seen. They promoted their color technology like somehow the sepia-looking images told a complex tale that grey could never communicate. Regardless, Ellen and I decided we would take the cheaply made poster's word for it.

Several minutes later, a young couple walked in. The mother was dressed more like a single woman on her way to a night club than an ultrasound. She was wearing hooker heels, a tight black shirt with shiny silver gothic writing all over it, and skinny jeans. She smiled kindly at us as they walked in, staring at Ellen's belly. She seemed to radiate sweetness, despite her rough exterior. The guy with her, I assumed to be the father, made Lil' Wayne look socially responsible. He had a large blob of green Indian ink on his face. I assumed it was some sort of tattoo that looked like a cross between the Versace logo and Ebola. I couldn't be certain, but it wasn't anything obvious like a tear drop. Nothing says "I hold my gun sideways" like a bad face tattoo. Judging by his arms, he had about fifty other similar quality tattoos to go with it. I only hoped he left enough room on his right peck for a really terrible portrait of his child.

"Do you guys know what you're having yet?" I asked.

"We find out today," she was clearly dying with anticipation. "Do you guys know?"

"We are having a girl," Ellen said sweetly. "How far along are you?"

"Thirty-four weeks."

The young mother smiled and nudged her lesser half as he stared off at the large flat panel television in the corner. There was a program on; its premise appeared to be simple enough: a panel of doctors discussing various medical topics. Each doctor had been clearly cast for obvious reasons, there was the good looking young man, the sexy young woman, the old doctor to give credibility, and a goofy guy that was the brunt of every joke. Today's topic, an investigation into the various lubrication products on the market and identifying which, if any, provided better orgasms.

The young mother giggled as she realized what he was watching and quickly nudged him again, "That's what got us in this mess."

He didn't respond, beyond looking extremely uncomfortable by the confession that they had sex. It was funny to me that a guy willing to tattoo "F-U-C-K" on his knuckles and wear his jeans halfway down his ass could blush like a schoolgirl over daytime television. The call of the administrator rescued him from any further humiliation.

It wasn't until they walked into the ultrasound room that I realized why they were here. This was the only affordable ultrasound option for them. Why else would they have not known the sex by now? Any OBGYN could have told them by now. Hell, I could have told them with an ultrasound machine and a dime sized spot of lube. Feeling bad for the mom, I could only imagine the worry she must have felt. For us, this was a fun afternoon and a t-shirt opportunity. For the uninsured it was the only option.

About ten minutes later they walked out. The mom was glowing, announcing "Healthy baby girl!"

"Congratulations!" Ellen and I said simultaneously.

"Thanks." Mom responded, while the ill-mannered father made his way to the door. His face showed slight traces of joy.

"Good luck!" she wished us as they left.

It was our turn. The technician led us to the dimly lit room. Inside, there were two more flat panel televisions, one looked to be about sixty plus inches and sat on the far wall directly across the room from what would soon be Ellen's large bed. This looked more like a bedroom from *MTV Cribs* than a medical office. The only things missing were the panel mirrors on the ceiling. As Ellen leaned back to de-robe, the tech got everything ready. With unprecedented efficiency, things were underway. The process started with the normal black and white 2D images we were used to. The tech walked us though all the basic anatomy stuff we had already seen.

"It's a girl, you guys know that, but I'm just confirming."

She typed "All Girl" onto the image as she printed it.

"I really hope you're right about us having a girl," Ellen joked. "We've already bought everything."

What about "All Girl" led her to believe that this may in fact be a boy? Did she go into this pregnancy expecting there to be problems identifying sex? Did my mother leak baby picture of me I hadn't seen. Something humiliating I'm sure, maybe me playing in the snow naked, with a particularly clitoral looking penis, struggling through ten below Celsius shrinkage?

Abby was only a thick French accent, a leotard and an ugly clown away from being the next Cirque De Soleil show. She was a contortionist, with one hand blocking one side of her face while the sole of her foot pressed against the other. The technician tried to get Abby to move, but she was stubborn. From the obscured view we could see that she looked like me, but had Ellen's personality. The technician agreed. As we waited for Abby to give us a clear shot of her face, the technician traveled around the belly, mapping out Abby's body. This gave me time to get answers to nagging questions like "Does she have a tail?"

In a last ditch effort, Ellen got out of bed, doing lunges and squats, hoping to shuffle Abby around. Alas, we had exhausted all of our time. We even moved into ten minutes of overtime, hoping Abby would give up a single glimpse. One good shot of her face. This little girl had a talent for telling a story and wasn't going to give away the plot. She only gave us enough to justify the $99, half a face with a finger in front of the exposed side, puckered lips and squinting eyes. The other side was hidden behind the sole of her foot. Nothing could hide that she looked just like her Daddy. I was starting to fall in love, but not enough to buy a mug in the gift shop.

Though the third trimester was supposed to be the most physically taxing, emotion was where Ellen's vulnerability now lied. Unfortunately, one of the newest and more disturbing side effects of pregnancy played off that weakness: third trimester advice. The third trimester was when people "started getting real." Probably because they suspected that small doses of stress wouldn't adversely affect the baby at this point. Now they could actually be honest.

People said crazy, terrifying things to pregnant women during the third trimester. One of the worst was: "You could go at any time." As if the thought of having a baby within twelve weeks wasn't scary enough. Let's up the ante and introduce the possibility of an incubator and maybe even jaundice. Abby could come out looking like a miniature Lindsey Lohan baking in her tanning bed.

Another handy story was: "I hemorrhaged when I delivered my placenta. I nearly bled to death on the table." This was helpful in distracting the new mom from her freshly pushed baby so she could concentrate on things like not hemorrhaging. Meanwhile, I would be left to fixate on the baby's wobbling unsupported head as it scaled Mount Nip-More looking for colostrum.

Last but not least, my personal favorite: "I tore from the base of my vagina to the extreme edge of my ass." Good to know that the destruction of childbirth wasn't only limited to the vagina. The ass was also vulnerable. What a great day that would be. We would get to meet our beautiful new daughter and make my wife's body more efficient by merging the vagina and ass into a dual purpose "vaginass." No more differentiating between doing number one and number two. She'd get to have a number three every time.

Even the medical staff we encountered, who dealt with pregnant women daily, didn't know any better. During a routine ultrasound, one technician asked if Ellen was going the natural route. When Ellen replied positively, the tech shook her head discouragingly. "I had a natural birth with my first child, and it was the dumbest thing I've ever done."

I developed a theory that pregnancy was like a hurricane. A couple of years after it was over you had no memory of it. The meds probably helped that even further. It was amnesia, and it was necessary. If women actually remembered childbirth, the earth's population would be extinct in a single generation. It was mind boggling that people rebuilt New Orleans months after hurricane Katrina. Equally, it boggles the mind that women had babies eighteen months apart. Just as the vaginass separated back into its two key components, capable of both bowel movements and sex through completely separate orifices, they were ready to go again. This also explained the complete lack of empathy for currently pregnant women. They simply didn't remember how terrified they were by those very same horror stories.

Women weren't the only ones exposed to the alarming repercussions of childbirth. Men were too. For men, the foreboding came by way of one single sadistic statement: "I hope you enjoyed having sex." Sadly, I couldn't remember.

Abstinence sucked, and I was feeling the stress that accompanied not having sex on a regular basis. It's not that we couldn't make time. Ellen and I would crawl into bed together every night. When I looked at Ellen lying next to me, she looked more beautiful than the day we met. Even so, the overwhelming urge was always dismissed. Even if I had been willing to initiate sex, and risk killing Abby, I would not have been willing to scale Pillow Mountain.

Pillow Mountain was a developing mountain range on a fault line cutting through the center of our bed. Each week it would climb higher, spreading further into my small sleepy village to the east. Why did anyone need so many pillows? It was a design flaw of pregnancy, Ellen's body could no longer support itself. It needed to be propped up, like a fancy multi-tiered cake. Otherwise, parts would collapse under their own weight. Originally, it started with a small sliver of a pillow called "*The Wedge.*" It looked like a foamy doorjamb that was placed underneath her hip. Later, a larger body pillow was added to keep her on her left side. Ellen explained that, while you were pregnant, sleeping on your left side was the key to a solid night's rest for you and your developing baby. Sleeping on your right side was attempting suicide.

My fondest memories of Pillow Mountain were about midway through its development, when it was about the same size as Ellen. Every time I turned the corner to our bedroom I would be momentarily startled by what looked like a body under the covers of our bed. During the installation of our hardwood floors, I found new ways to amuse myself with the deceptively suspicious looking pillow figure. Plumbers and carpenters would always stare nervously at the bed as I led them through the bedroom to the master bath. I found great joy in lowering my voice to a whisper as we moved closer the bedroom. Careful never to make eye contact with the pillows, which may as well have been a chalk outline. Once we moved into the bathroom, just an eye shot away from the pillows (which I had purposely arranged to look like a body minutes before the crew arrived), I would quickly raise my voice to normal speaking levels.

As Pillow Mountain gained altitude, our white duvet climbed as well, and covered the top like a blanket of white snow while I lay shivering naked at its base. Eventually, even Pillow Mountain wasn't enough, and Ellen tossed and turned throughout the night as if the constant shuffling of our puppies crated in the corner of our bedroom wasn't disruptive enough. When Ellen wasn't climbing out of bed to pee, she was huffing, puffing and slapping her arms against the bed in frustration. If I couldn't get a good night's sleep now, what was it going to be like once Abby arrived?

Pillows and noise weren't the only new additions to our once sexy bedroom. Like a baby bomb shelter, we had supplies stacked against every wall as we waited for laborgeddon. During the mornings, as I left for work, I would stumble in the darkness, trying not to wake Ellen. Wading through the small walking paths that winded through the piles and piles of "must haves." Every nook and cranny of our room was filled with delivery supplies like car seats, pillows from a previous Pillow Mountain avalanche, suitcases, stacks of paperwork, blankets, and even portable sound systems. Had I been compelled to strike a match and light a candle, I'm sure a fire marshal would have come crashing through our bedroom window.

Even our king size bed was reduced to a giant crib by extending into a "*Co-sleeper.*" This was where the newest member of our estrogen filled cabana was going to hang out. At least until Ellen was reasonably convinced that SIDS wasn't looming in the shadows of our nursery. This would basically eliminate any risk of sex or masturbation for at least the next six months. Goodbye bedroom, hello west wing of the nursery.

WEEK 32:

BLEACH

I stared at the 3D ultrasound displayed by my digital picture frame on my desk. Abby was frozen inside the 3D amber image like a mosquito preserved in tree sap from a thousand years ago. I was still trying to comprehend that the cute button nose, tiny puffy lips, and squinting eyes belonged to my daughter. The 3D image wasn't some Pixar creation. This cute little girl was Abby, curled up inside my wife's belly.

Some predictions about Abby were easier to make than others. Ellen is half Greek. I am half Lebanese. So Abby would probably be covered in a thick curly black coat of hair when she was born. But would she be a quiet baby like Ellen and (believe it or not) me? Would she stay quiet like Ellen or evolve into a complete pain in the ass like I did? Maybe she wouldn't be anything like either one of us. Maybe she would be a devil child like her Aunt Trina? That would be difficult.

Trina is the best sister-in-law anyone could ever hope for. She is loving, kind, smart, sensitive, beautiful, but by all accounts completely oblivious to her surroundings. To be fair, I tend to hyper-focus on my surroundings and the constant threat of any number of possible natural disasters, animal attacks, and any potentially dangerous nearby inanimate objects. However, my observation of Trina's absent mindedness wasn't just a result of my compulsions, Ellen and her mother, Karen, completely agreed.

About five years ago Trina's fiancé, an equally great person named Jeff, was a fighter pilot. He had recently survived ejecting from his exploding harrier. As a result, the military decided, as his reward, to ground him permanently and send him to Iraq. Rather than leaving Trina to live alone, we asked her if she would like to stay with us until Jeff returned. Trina accepted. I had never had a sibling of my own, but I always dreamt of what it might be like. We were thrilled. Ellen got to see her sister daily, and I got to have un-moderated daily conversations with a woman who offered no threat of cutting off sex.

Living with Trina was a lot of fun. The good times far outweighed the stress related to the new breasts I had developed as a result of the higher estrogen levels in our home. The two bitches, Moochie and Pygmy, were happy as well. Just like me, they needed constant attention and Trina was able to help lighten the demands on Ellen.

One thing we failed to consider when asking her to live with us was that Trina had just spent two years stationed in Micronesia, serving in the Peace Corps. Most of her days were spent eating with rats, sleeping with bugs and waiting for local boy's penises to shimmy through her windowless hut while she slept, "Night Crawlers" they were called by the locals. As opposed to sex offenders here in America. Those guys know how to get the ladies. Why waste time throwing pebbles at a window while juggling a hand full of flowers. Simply peek your penis through the bedroom window like a submarine's periscope. In the history of Micronesia, had anyone ever managed to get laid that way?

You couldn't spend two years eating rice off wooden planks in a giant sandbox surrounded by a night sky full of stray penises without developing some idiosyncrasies. Trina's came through in her perception of what was normal. Particularly, her laidback lifestyle versus what she perceived as our little slice of Alcatraz. I remember one day coming home after work, Trina was sitting down in our living room comfortably watching TV in her PJ's. I smiled, said hello and removed my shoes. 'Man it feels warm in here, I hope our A/C isn't on its way out,' I thought. It was 20 years old and struggled in the hot southern summer. I walked into the family room and found the back door wide open with a large pile of leaves scattered across the living room. Our two white malti-poos lay baking in the hot sun. They were covered in bits of crap they had spent most of the afternoon rolling around in, while waiting for the next squirrel to terrorize.

"Trina?! Why is the back door open?"

"Huh? Oh I guess must have forgotten to close it, sorry," she said, staring blankly at the television.

I thought about what she had said, fighting the urge to have a reaction. I stared at Pygmy as she squinted back at me across the sun drenched yard. She looked at me in way that said "I know, Daddy, I know." I couldn't help but wonder if maybe tomorrow Trina would "forget" to close the front door. Or maybe she would "forget" that she shouldn't feed dogs chocolate covered raisins.

"Trina, could you please try very hard not to forget to close exterior doors to the house in the future?"

"I'm sorry," she said calmly from the living room. "You guys have so many rules, I can't keep track of them all!"

Over the eighteen months that Trina spent with us, many new rules unfolded. Now, years later, most of those arguments have dissolved away, and instead I tend to remember all of the fun we had together. Like the bad times, most of the rules have been long forgotten as well. Only the few she struggled with the most come to mind. Rule Number 1: Please close exterior doors of our home. Rule Number 23: Please don't drive your new car into things. Rule Number 25: Please don't back your new car into things. Last but not least, Rule Number 48: Please don't pour bleach across the family room carpet as you walk from the guest bathroom to the kitchen.

Maybe Trina helped prepare me for fatherhood. She may have been God's test run. He had to see if I could make it a whole eighteen months without packing my shit in the middle of the night and heading for some Caribbean island. If my time with Trina, combined with Ellen's current pregnancy, had taught me anything it was to let go of the little things. Which is much easier said than done. But at least maybe now I was ready for the real thing, the advanced course, the eighteen year curriculum of Abby.

It was time for our next midwife visit. I would have called it an appointment, but that seemed far too formal and insinuated a degree of thoroughness I didn't feel was present. It still amazed me that insurance covered this, not that there was very much expense to cover (which was probably all the explanation necessary). This time we were going to meet the third of four possible midwives and Nina was her name-o.

So far, in the race to be the best midwife, Teresa held a commanding lead. We had only met Sunset briefly during the tour. She seemed nice, but I hadn't felt the calm demeanor with her that I had seen with Teresa. I was interested to see how Nina would rank. As before, we waited patiently in our room. Unlike the OBGYN, midwives were apparently fine with leaving us alone with the world's greatest sex chair. I theorized that this was actually a strategy for getting us to have sex and spur on labor. When the knock on the door happened, it was followed by a tall, attractive and incredibly athletic looking woman in her late forties.

With a strong Spanish accent, she greeted us, "Ellen, I don't believe we've met, and you must be James. Hello," she began feeling around Ellen's belly while smiling at me politely. "Great, she feels like she's in a good position."

She went on to listen to the heart and take measurements of my wife's belly, "So, how has everything been going?" she asked, winding up her thirty-second detailed assessment of our child's health.

"Are you going to do an ultrasound or check the cervix?" I asked while Ellen rolled her eyes.

"Nope," she said turning her head from side to side as she smiled at Ellen. "As long as everything looks fine there's no reason; maybe as we get closer to the due date."

My question was obviously irrelevant. Nothing on the planet made you feel more like a "dish liquid husband" than a condescending midwife with her back to you. A dish liquid husband is the worst thing you could ever be. Any man that has ever seen a dish liquid commercial has had their ego chipped away ever so slightly, and probably without having even detected it.

The demographic of any household cleaning product is usually the mother, I'll agree to that. Therefore, it makes sense that she be portrayed as an attractive, fit, thirty-something. Also, it is logical that she understands the brand and why it is critical to everyday life. The husband, on the other hand, is cast as a typically balding, overweight, do-nothing. Often, he's found thumbing through the sports section of the newspaper or slouched over a bowl of potato chips in sweatpants watching a football game. His role is to generate filth or be filthy himself, and this was where our product would come into play.

He is oblivious to his surroundings, while his hot unappreciated wife of clearly superior intellect cleans the mess surrounding him. She smiles and picks up his disgusting nacho plate covered in scraps of excessively microwaved cheese and crusty dried-up salsa. But as she walks to the sink, she always rolls her eyes then demonstrates in thirty seconds, how effective the product is, even against the giant grub of a man she suffers through marriage with.

That was how I felt. Every question I asked generated a polite smile by Nina and a subtle acknowledgement by my wife, like some clever code of condescension that women learned from having been pregnant. A small nod could communicate: "I know, he's dumb, he understands nothing, but it would be easier for me if we humored him with an answer." Nina answered in the most trivializing way possible, only sparing me the indignity of speaking in baby talk.

"Don't you worry. Your job is just to stay calm. Be there for her. Momma and I will guide you through everything."

WEEKS 33 TO 34:

PARADISA

As Abby's arrival grew closer, I began to collect the most cherished memories of my childhood and think of ways for me to share them with her. One of my most precious memories revolved around my father and *Lego*. When I was a young child, my father worked for the predominant Canadian meat packing plant. He worked the nightshift and occasionally he brought me with him. While he was off doing whatever it was he did, he would leave me in his office with various parts from freshly slaughtered pigs and cows, usually hooves and ears. I would stare at the fleshy cross section of the latest appendage and count the rings of flesh like it was a tree.

Sometimes, when I was really lucky, my father would walk in with the large brass ring from a cow's nose. That was the Holy Grail of workplace toys. The rings were hinged on one quadrant and as they were pried apart the opposite side would reveal two sharp points. Whenever my father left the room, I always tried to see if I could pierce it through my skin. The nose was too painful, though I tried, but if I pinched the skin on the back of my hand I could come close. Sometimes I would draw blood, but not much more than a spot. Unfortunately, those evenings were rare and, for the vast majority of the time I stayed at home with my mother and did what most young children did at night, sleep. My father would come home at 6am while my mother left for her retail job, and by 8am I was already jumping on the foot of my father's bed shouting.

My father quickly learned that two hours of sleep a night wasn't going to cut it. He needed a way to distract me. So every morning, he would get home from work at the crack of dawn, nauseous from coffee, exhausted from a twelve-hour nightshift. Still, without exception, each morning he would pull out my *Tupperware* tub of second hand *Lego* and put together something for me. It was our ritual. I would hop out of bed, every day, like it was Christmas to see what he had come up with. I laid there for hours appreciating his work, in complete awe of his sophisticated *Lego* skill level. I spent the next couple of hours trying to re-create the exact same toy by reverse engineering his design like some alien space ship by military scientists in Area 51. Eventually, when Dad was rested enough to give me his undivided attention, he would crawl out of bed and join in. These were important times in my life, they had a deep impact on me, and they defined what I hoped to be as a father to Abby.

My newest obsession became researching toys and what the world of *Lego* had to offer Abby. Five minutes into a *Lego Store* reconnaissance mission, I learned the answer: nothing. A quick Q and A with the 18 year old *Lego* representative confirmed as much. Once home, I logged on to *Lego.com* and looked around.

Relieved to find a "Girls" tab, I enthusiastically clicked it and found "*Belleville*", *Lego* for little girls framed in pretty pink boxes. The 83 piece "*Playful Puppy*" was the top seller. The 54 piece "*Horse Jump*" and the colossal, out of stock, 209 piece "*Horse Stable*" took second and third place honors. I hit the back button on my browser to be certain I hadn't accidentally clicked the special needs link.

To put things in perspective, when clicking the "Exclusives" link I was brought to a page filled with boy friendly sets like the 3,803 piece "*Death Star*" and the 2,231 piece "*Fire Station*". Never had I been so disappointed in a toy company. Hell, I was disappointed in the whole country of Denmark. Somehow I just assumed a sleek European nation would have been more progressive. Most people thought the Danish were most famous for things like, say, Danishes... but not to me. Until now, I had felt Europe's most generous gift to America wasn't a French tiara-wearing copper statue. It was *Lego*.

I began to research why Denmark, specifically, *Lego* had failed Abby so terribly. I wanted to think it was just a cultural thing. It would have been easy to blame it on their monarchy, clinging to the old ways, believing that all young women should attend finishing school. The girls were in a library somewhere practicing their curtsy, while balancing a book on their head. Meanwhile, all the Danish boys were reconstructing their goofy looking European trucks with *Lego*. It was a boys club: Brits had the Freemasonry and Danes had *Lego*.

Though I had clearly solved the mystery of the missing pink *Lego* dollhouse, I decided to dig a little deeper. I found out I wasn't the only father who wanted my daughter to excel in math and have enough spatial intelligence to load a dishwasher beyond 18% capacity. The internet revealed others, others who sought the same answers I did and they had already uncovered the ugly truth, "*Paradisa*". *Paradisa* was a failed, six year run, of girl-friendly *Lego* in the mid-nineties. It wasn't the 2,220 piece dollhouse I longed for, but it at least demonstrated an effort. The Danes extended the olive branch to the *Barbie*-crazed girls of America, and it was ignored. It was a titanic failure and with it sank the possibility of getting *Lego* interpretations of *Disney's Beauty and the Beast* castle or *Barbie's* pink convertible. Hopefully, Abby wouldn't object to afternoon tea parties in the *Death Star*.

DUCK AND POTATO

S unday Morning, I crawled out of bed yearning for coffee. I was watching my weight, and had been fantasizing about my morning coffee since the night before when I passed on having a *Skinny Cow* ice cream sandwich for dessert. I went straight for the coffee maker. When it was up and brewing, I pulled out my *Parisian Crème Coffee Mate*. If my morning coffee wasn't as satisfying as a platter of tiramisu, I was pissed. For me, coffee was more like dessert from the previous evening simply rolling into the next day.

Priority number two: feeding the dogs. I reached into the pantry and pulled out a can of Duck and Potato dog food. Ellen was too busy for coffee and dogs. She was scattering everything she owned across the bed, preparing for her pregnancy picture appointment scheduled later that morning. Pygmy would eat duck and potato dog food for the rest of her life. Duck and potato were two of the five things she wasn't allergic too. The other three were water, tennis balls and air. If she were to eat, say, chicken while sitting on a human with hair, two of her more serious allergies, she would have tear stains darker than Robert Smith's eyeliner. Ironic, considering we bought a hypoallergenic dog to help reduce my own allergy issues. She actually shed less than I did. Unfortunately, a hairy half Lebanese man like me was probably the worst shedding breed of owner Pygmy could have picked for her own allergies.

The act of walking toward the cabinet that contained the electric can opener sent Pygmy into her usual quivering ritual. Sitting, shaking in the middle of our kitchen, like she was in an industrial freezer, Pygmy waited. Moochie, on the other hand, was prancing about in circles like Stevie Nicks around a campfire. Pygmy was the eater of the two. She would do anything for food. Her treats needed to be smaller than a dime, because she always swallowed them whole.

We were out of dry food; this morning would be a rare treat of delectable canned food. Spooning out two bowls of food, I prepared one for of each puppy. But instead of mashing the food into the bowls, like I normally would, I left it in larger clumps. Hoping it might be helpful in slowing Pygmy's pace, forcing her to approach it from one side. Biting off little hunks was preferred to vacuuming up the entire dish of crumbled food. Setting down the bowls, I walked over to the couch and sat back with my warm, oversized Superman mug of caffeinated sugar.

Sipping my coffee from across the room, I could see Pygmy wasn't biting off pieces as I had predicted. Instead, she was chomping down one giant can shaped piece. It was so large it hung out one side of her mouth as she tried gulping it back like a sea gull. It didn't make any sense to me: the food was the consistency of sticky rice. It couldn't support its own weight, and it certainly should have crumbled easily under the force of Pygmy's jaw. Something unusual was lodged in her food. Slowly, I stood up. Knowing that if she suspected I might try to take it from her, she would attempt to swallow it whole.

As I stood up, Pygmy immediately recognized that her food was at risk and, as predicted, she tried to force it down. As she did, her back legs spread out and her belly touched the floor like she was stretching. I knew she was choking. She fell onto her side and began moving her legs slowly like she was swimming through the air.

"PYGMY!"

By the time I got to her, she looked like she was having a seizure. Within seconds her eyes rolled back and she went completely limp. Flipping her onto her back, I began a scaled down version of a hybrid between the Heimlich maneuver and chest compressions. Pushing twice near the base of her little rib cage, I applied moderate force. She didn't respond. I yelled her name again and did two more compressions with significantly more force. Nothing happened. I knew I was running out of time. I did another compression, this one dangerously hard, realizing I was losing my little friend.

She slowly opened her eyes, lifted her head, and began chewing the dislodged mystery chunk. Again, I tried to fish it out of her mouth, and again she swallowed the damn thing. Pygmy gradually got up, and with her lightly wagging cotton ball tail pointing down, she moved back to her food dish to see if there was any food left.

"Pygmy just died!!!" I yelled as Ellen walked into the living room.

"What?"

I went on to explain what happened. Ellen was saddened to learn the howling she had mistaken to be the dogs, was actually me dropping to my knees like Charlton Heston at the end of *Planet of the Apes*. I could see her growing more upset as I continued to describe it. We were already supposed to have left for the photos. There was no way I was going anywhere without Pygmy.

Ellen begrudgingly left without me; I stayed home and watched over our little puppy. Pygmy walked towards me, where I sat on the kitchen floor, still by her bowl where she had blacked out.

We spent the rest of the afternoon lying on the couch while Ellen had her pictures taken. Pygmy nuzzled into my neck and the feeling of her breath made me want to cry. We were only weeks away from being parents to a newborn, and I couldn't even feed my dog without nearly killing it. How was I going to feed a baby? I imagined the anxiety I would feel in the coming weeks every time I had to feed Pygmy. We were only weeks away from the delivery and I was still nowhere near ready to be a father yet.

WEEKS 36 TO 37:

PEDIATRICIAN

llen and I argued about vaccinations since about the time we settled on a name. It was the latest masochistic go-to topic for either of us when we felt the subconscious need to burden ourselves with additional stress. Ellen read everything she could find on the subject. Nearly once a week, I would get an email from "*BabyCenter*, stating: "Ellen thinks you might find this article interesting." I knew what that meant: Ellen was sending me my latest batch of homework. I knew that, seconds after crossing the threshold of our front door that afternoon, the questioning would begin.

"Did you read the article I sent you?" she dare not say the title, in fear that I may somehow fake my way through the conversation.

"Yes, it was a great article. I'm glad we both agree that Abby should be vaccinated," I would say, consistently. The problem with consistency was, in an environment laced with hormones, what once came off as support sprinkled with mild interest was now seen as arrogance… or worse, some sort of challenge.

The problem was that each new article she passed along completely contradicted a previous one. One article could be summarized as "Vaccines are fine, just spread them out." While the next would conclude "Many vaccines haven't been around long enough to know long term effects." As soon as we managed to unite on a way forward, I was downloading the next article: "Vaccine studies regarding Autism have no scientific evidence to support them." What all of these articles really told me was that I needed to stop trying to speak on the subject of inoculation.

Thankfully, the time came for us to seek out a Pediatrician's opinion. For those of you new to fatherhood, this is NOT a foot doctor, it's a baby doctor. Finally, the climactic battle I had been waiting for was actually going to happen: measles versus autism.

We visited two doctors on two different days, and both were nice enough. They both met the new segregation standard for waiting rooms. The "Sick" were quarantined on one side, separated by a glass wall from the "Healthy." I'd imagined the anxiety I would have felt as a child, walking down the hall towards the "Life" and "Death" doors. Door number one meant you would enjoy your summer frolicking in playgrounds and eating fudgesicles, while door number two meant you would be hooked up to an IV for the rest of the summer, pale and friendless. Come to think of it, who was I kidding? My parents wouldn't have brought me to the doctor as a child. Hell, even if they wanted to, we lived in rural Newfoundland. I don't think we even had a pediatrician.

Ellen brought several pages of material with her to our appointments, essentially for testing potential doctors. Surprisingly, one actually scored high enough to get a passing grade from Ellen, but he didn't get a happy face sticker: those were reserved solely for midwives. The pediatrician was not only a professor at a local medical school; he also helped develop the HPV vaccine. In Ellen's mind, this was the next best thing to having read a book on vaccines.

We walked to the small Argentinean man's office. He spoke about the upcoming world cup match while sporting their blue colors under his white coat. What he didn't discuss was the half a dozen nationally circulated magazines that were framed in the hallway leading to his office proclaiming his greatness in the field of vaccinations. His knowledge on the subject of children's medicine would be hard to de-base, even for Ellen.

He was clearly excited and went on to explain that he was heading to Colorado for several weeks and that we were his last appointment. He smiled a lot and spoke quickly, I liked him already. Within the first ten minutes, he gave us a complete summary of where we were in the pregnancy and all of his responsibilities up until the end of our stay at the hospital. As he finished, he quickly flipped through books from his bookcase behind him and asked us if we had read any of them. Ellen, like a prowling lioness, saw her chance to strike.

"Actually, I have," she said shuffling her papers like she was preparing to make a presentation.

"I've read Ina May's *Guide to Breastfeeding* and Dr. Sears' *The Vaccine Book.*"

These selections may have seemed innocent enough, but these were not just statements of fact. Instead, they were cleverly veiled questions waiting for a response.

"They're good books," he replied. "I am very pro breastfeeding."

He continued to describe his position on various subjects. He highlighted every major philosophy I had listened to Ellen present over the past eight months. Reaching behind himself, as he spoke, he pulled out the book Ellen had read by Dr. Sears and laid it on his desk.

"Dr. Sears isn't anti-vaccine, he's pro vaccine. Doctor Sears has it right, so don't worry about that criminal in London that published the bogus report because he was being pressured to find a link to Autism," he said while pulling out a four inch binder and flipping to a photocopied article from the UK.

Once the doctor finished narrating the encyclopedia of inoculation, and Ellen finished examining the spines of his books for wear, he presented an opportunity for Ellen to continue her questioning. She drilled him on various subjects, including baby-administered poisons like Vitamin K and eye ointment, résumé's for the answering service, and the route he would use to get to the hospital. Somehow, the doctor not only answered the questions, but did so enthusiastically.

Ellen's assault was ruthless, but we left with the answers she needed to tough questions like:

"Our child is crawling at 0.274 miles/hour towards you, and you are exactly 18 feet away moving at 3.1 miles/hours from the opposite direction with a fist full of MMR vaccinations. How old will our child be when she develops Autism?"

Finally, for the first time since firing our OBGYN, we had a doctor back on the payroll.

Ellen had another midwife visit this week and, as usual, they rotated. The midwives' delivery schedule rotated every couple of days. There was no guaranteeing who would actually deliver Abby, so it was important for us to get to know each of them. This time, the appointment was with Sunset. We hadn't seen her since our midwife tour and I was going to have to miss today's appointment because of work. I didn't really care, Sunset was my least favorite of the midwives so far. I couldn't put my finger on why. Most likely it was due to having met her when I had little respect for the profession. Midwives were little more than hippies to me at the time. Since then, I had slowly come around and nearly elevated them to vaginal chiropractor status. I acted disappointed when Ellen called me at work to let me know she was on her way there.

"Baby, I'm really sorry, that I'm going to have to miss today's midwife appointment."

Oddly enough, by the end of the day I was already feeling guilty, like I had missed one of Abby's recitals. I decided that once I was home, I would study some of our baby books to make up for the missed appointment.

When we realized Ellen was pregnant, I went out that week and bought several baby books for us to read. Every Sunday, from the couch, I would read Abby's development in the coming week, out loud, while Ellen made French toast. We did this throughout her pregnancy until we fell off the wagon around week 22. We became less interested when compelling narrative on the baby's development was replaced with details surrounding the imminent collapse of Ellen's vagina.

Amazing developmental statements found in previous chapters like: "Today, your baby has begun to develop kidneys," were soon replaced with, "You will notice increased mucus from the vagina over the next few weeks. Pinkish brown discharge is normal, while green or dark brown needs to be reported to your doctor."

It had been so long since we read from those books that I decided to simply brush up on the essential baby stuff. The details were summed up on the first page of every chapter. That would be the easiest way for me to avoid all the gory details of the day by day stuff.

Baby Book Lunar Month 1 Tip - Avoid illness. Did crippling food poisoning count?

Baby Book Lunar Month 2 - Avoid caffeine, cigarettes, alcohol and drugs. She did sip my beer, wine and coffee. I assumed it was the "you are a bastard for drinking this in front of me" tax.

Baby Book Lunar Month 3 - Do not fall or pass out. Finally, criteria we managed to pass. Unless, of course, Ellen had just been keeping her daily falls a secret. She'd probably collapsed endless times by now, as she normally did, particularly after having stubbed her toe. Now that she couldn't see where they were, it seemed even more likely. If she hadn't stubbed her toe at least once over the past nine months, it would easily be the longest consecutive period of having not done so in her life.

Baby Book Lunar Month 4 - In Russia it was believed that if a woman had a bad or long labor, they had been cheating. Noted.

Baby Book Lunar Month 5 - Lie on your left side, use pillows to support your legs. Pass, Pillow Mountain supported every flap of skin she had.

Baby Book Lunar Month 6 - Sumatra midwives cut the umbilical with a flute so the baby will have a good voice. Noted, don't forget to pack a flute in our labor bags.

Baby Book Lunar Month 7 - Mayan women of the Yucatan would share horror stories during pregnancy. We had that one covered. You didn't have to be a four foot tall native dressed in a woolen rainbow to be insensitive. North Americans followed this tradition as well.

Baby Book Lunar Month 8 – In Colonial America, an axe was used to "cut" the pain during labor. Also releasing horses from the stable helped. Noted, don't forget to pack an axe, preferably in the flute bag.

Baby Book Lunar Month 9 – Collect music to bring to the delivery room, it will help mom relax. Crap! I forgot the music!

By Ellen's request, I was supposed to download the soundtrack to The Crucible. This film, though she'd claimed it was the book, deeply impacted her as a tween. More accurately, Daniel Day Lewis probably impacted her multiple times in her pre-pubescent fantasies. She was pretty much obsessed with the guy. I didn't care, if the score made the birth more relaxing for her, so be it.

I did a quick search on iTunes to see what I could find. As I looked at the song titles, I noticed track 14: "Abigail Disappears." I'd been duped, Ellen's fabricated divinity dream of a daughter named Abby was just a heretical sex dream. Of course, I found this out after we told the world that Abby was going to be Abby.

Whatever, I just needed to pack our bag. Pillow? Check. Flute? Check. Axe? Check. Soundtrack of lies? Check. If this turned out to be a particularly long labor, I might need to pay Daniel Day Lewis a visit.

As the delivery grew closer, Ellen decided that we should expose our two dogs to our friend's babies. Why not? I thought. The used baby clothes, car seats and all of the items with which we equipped the nursery seemed to go unnoticed by them. So we invited over two couples who weren't afraid of getting a little puppy slobber on their babies.

Pygmy, though she was a little hyper, seemed to do better than Moochie. Pygmy was more affectionate and was satisfied to lick the baby's toes and fingers. Moochie, on the other hand, was less comfortable and released unprovoked, oddly timed yelp-barks. When she would simmer down, something would trigger the "Reset" button and it would start all over again.

I tried to offer helpful suggestions. Perhaps if we were to kill Moochie and make an example of her, Pygmy could be salvaged. Ellen wasn't interested. She loved Moochie, even if Moochie was clearly inferior to Pygmy. Though I joked, as always, there was a degree of truth (and history) to what I said.

Pets in my household growing up never had much of a chance. The first pet I remember losing to my parents was a rabbit. I don't remember its name or what sex it was. I just remember that it lived in a box with one side open, free to roam our basement as it pleased. When I would get bored, as five year olds do, I would go downstairs and feed it carrots and cabbage. I would try to hug it against its will and tickle its back paws so that it would hop across the dingy basement floor.

One day, I came home from school and Dad met me at the door smiling with his hand behind his back.

"Guess what I found?"

I dropped my backpack and waited for what would surely be the greatest gift on earth.

"A lucky rabbit's foot!" he said dangling it in front of me.

I was elated, he had even made it into a keychain by pushing a key-ring through the skin between the tendon and the bone.

"Watch this," he said as he grabbed the small white tendon that stuck out where the leg had been severed and pulled on it. As he did, the whole foot began to extend. I stared at my new rabbit's foot for the rest of the day, looking at the cross section of the leg, smelling the meat and pulling the tendon so it would knock over my carefully erected GI Joes.

Years later, between fits of laughter, my father explained to me that my rabbit had chewed up our new ten-man tent, which was also stored in our basement. When he discovered the damage, he slaughtered, skinned and gutted the rabbit. That evening, we ate my pet rabbit as stew. I don't remember eating it, though my father assured me that they told me. As I ate it, he said I offered no reaction, just staring at the paw as I ate.

"It wasn't half bad for domesticated rabbit," he summed up, giggling with pride. "I do remember the smell of the little rabbit's foot," my father told me. They eventually had to throw it out for that very reason he explained, and that I had cried, asking for another lucky foot to replace it. He said for weeks I would question cashiers every time we went into a store to find out if they sold rabbits.

This, along with the other half dozen pets I was robbed of throughout my childhood, changed me. My unreasonable fear of very reasonable risks leaves me extremely overprotective. Dog parks, groomers, boarding, and my own international travel are approached each time like they are my final moments together with my beloved dogs. It was important to me that we took every step necessary to make sure the dogs weren't going to be a problem with Abby. I didn't want to find myself in the same place I was as a child, losing another beloved pet. Even worse, this time it wouldn't be a ten-man tent getting chewed up, it would be Abby.

PRESCRIPTION SEX

Finally, it was time to meet the fourth and final midwife, Dot. Just like the other midwives, Dot did her quick belly inspection, heartbeat check, snapped off her gloves and asked if we had any questions.

"How will we know Ellen's starting labor?" I asked, having heard stories of women who didn't realize they'd been in labor until they delivered a baby in a toilet.

Dot went on for what seemed like days, explaining how rare it was to have a baby in the car on the way to a hospital. This assured me that this was exactly what would happen to Abby. She gave personal accounts of having been the midwife for women with labor so intense it could have easily resulted in delivering on route, but it never did. She also highlighted dozens of cases of the much more common false alarm. She suggested that before we did anything we should call the hospital, and one of the midwives would call us back. They would talk to Ellen, and then determine if it was time to come in. If we called after hours, we would be directed to an answering service and they would contact the midwife on call that night for us.

Waiting while some "middle-wife" dispatcher passed our message on to an actual midwife struck me as a pretty inefficient system. Shouldn't we have been provided a direct number on a laminated business card designed to survive the slimy, gushy event leading up to the call? I expected to be provided a red phone like the one Commissioner Gordon used to call Batman, one that would light up as it rang. Not some number to an operating service. Not to mention, checking the cervix over the phone seemed particularly un-scientific. I wished I had the power to sense a thinning cervix simply by listening to a woman's voice. I wouldn't need to worry about my wife faking an orgasm. Though, realistically, there was little to no likelihood of that, Ellen was well past the point of caring enough to fake an orgasm for my sake.

Dot went on to explain that women's confusion regarding labor was due to doctors who consistently allowed people to come to the hospital too early. They would then break their patient's water and drug them to the point that they never had a chance to feel a contraction. She made it sound like there was a dry erase board hanging in the hospital lunch room, where doctors, like car salesman, would compete to knock out the most babies by month's end.

The whole phantom labor thing scared me. Over the course of the pregnancy, I began to lose trust in Ellen's ability to gauge her body. Even though she'd often claimed that she was very much in tune with her body, she left a very different impression. Statements such as "What does heartburn feel like" tipped me off. Just a week ago, one of our friends described what a Braxton

Hicks contraction felt like. Not two hours later, Ellen looked at me and said "Feel that?" placing my hand on her belly "I'm having my first Braxton Hicks contraction."

Once Dot finished up her forty five minute explanation of "How to know you're in labor," she ended with, "…if you haven't started by forty-one weeks, the midwives here have been known to write a prescription for sex to induce labor."

Ellen quickly laughed, "I told him I was going to make him at forty weeks whether he wanted it or not."

I stared towards the window acting like there was something of interest out there, like I hadn't heard them. I immediately wondered if I could find a doctor to write the same prescription for Ellen after the baby arrived.

Take penis twice daily with porn and vodka. 7,300 refills.

I knew how that would go over. Probably about the same way her baby crushing, fluid gushing prescription for sex had with me.

WEEK 39:

DID YOU FEEL THAT?!

E llen and I were in survival mode, pretty much living in fear of her first contraction. I feared anything that could be the catalyst to set our little science experiment into motion. Normal things, like heat from the sun, worried me. Walking across the parking lot to the grocery store on Sunday, I remember thinking it was too hot and that we shouldn't have come. About halfway between the car and the store, Ellen put her hands on her belly and slowed down. She may as well have been strapped with explosives with her thumb on the detonator.

"What!" I yelled paralyzed in a half squatted position so I could look her in the eyes. "What is it?!" I shouted loudly, looking like I had just wandered onto a mine field.

"It's just a Braxton Hick's, baby. It happens every time I walk now," she replied, her belly tight like an over-inflated basketball.

"Don't move," I pleaded. "Wait till it passes." I looked around the parking lot for a motorized *Rascal* for her to ride to the front door. There were none to be found, probably all buried under obese women who had lost the will to walk.

I remembered the panicked husband from the birthing classes. I understood his fear, why he lived in anxiety of the smallest of movements as his wife sat in Beverly's old rocker. I tentatively followed Ellen as we inched our way closer to the entrance of the store.

When we entered the store, I realized Ellen was in even graver danger than she had been in sunlight. The cramped produce section worried me. It looked like a frenzied ant trail of middle aged women fighting over a dead beetle. Just in front of us was a woman, blind to the world around her, carefully picking the most appealing stocks of broccoli, as if her ungrateful family would even notice. I watched her spin around with reckless abandon after selecting her final stock of broccoli. She was looking for the nearest roll of produce bags, her elbows flailing wildly. I could feel myself tensing up, ready to throw myself between her and Ellen like a rookie cop diving to take a bullet for his partner.

Advancing carefully through the anarchy of the produce department to the open deli section, I recognized a completely different threat. Shoppers now free of the congested organics section were able to pick up speed around the open freezers of the meat section. We were surrounded by clueless shoppers reading grocery lists as they pushed carts. They may as well have been drunk drivers. I jumped in front of Ellen with my cart as soon as the opportunity arose. Leading the way, I was ready to collide as necessary with any cart that posed a threat.

As we continued shopping, even benign aisles like the cereal aisle were problematic. Ellen stopped to get her favorite *Kashi* morning cereal, pressing her belly against the boxes as she reached for the top shelf. Danger loomed, before I knew it, a careless couple had pushed their cart immediately between Ellen and me, mere inches behind her back. They didn't say excuse me, and they clearly didn't think that Ellen might turn around tripping over their cart, killing both her and our unborn child. Instead, they just passed by slowly in silence, without even so much as a courtesy grunt.

I clearly struggled with elevated levels of preemptive protective instincts. As we entered the parking lot, I watched cars and monitored their speeds. I looked at accelerating vehicles as they passed by at thirty miles an hour. I wanted to follow them to their parking spots as they got out of the vehicle and force them down to the ground under a fury of punches. I wanted to rip out their throats like Patrick Swayze in *Roadhouse*. I imagined myself trying to do the same, unsuccessfully, my fingers slipping as I struggled to grip their sweaty double chin under the sweltering summer heat.

Anyone that drove faster than me was a lunatic, while driving even slightly slower than me lumped them into the "accident causing idiots" category. Abby needed to stay put just a little longer. I needed time to have a "Caution: Violently Over-Protective Father On Board" sticker made for my back window.

The closer we got to our delivery date, the more I badgered Ellen with questions. Questions like "Are you leaking and is it Green?" or "Are you having a contraction?" like somehow she'd forget to mention it. The worst thing I could have learned was that when a woman's water broke, it could be any number of colors. And each was potentially symptomatic of a completely different problem. Green amniotic fluid, for example, terrified me. It wasn't ectoplasm, like one might think, and it didn't mean she was giving birth to a ghost. Instead, it meant that the baby had done number two in the womb. That wasn't a good thing. Then there was red amniotic fluid, which was never properly explained to me, so I was left to assume red as a result of blood. This was also probably not a good thing. Another possibility that scared me was the gradual leak. It was like some pipe under the sink that went unnoticed for weeks, once discovered leaving you with little choice but to demolish half the kitchen. Every time Ellen needed to pee, I held my breath waiting to find out if she had sprung a leak.

"Well, what happened?" I would ask, frustrated that Ellen hadn't recognized the obvious need to continuously update me on her watertight integrity.

"I just needed to pee!" she was clearly annoyed that I cared for her and Abby's well being.

I would stare at her suspiciously, waiting for some indication that she wasn't one hundred percent certain. I would glance at her crotch just to make sure there was no wet spot. Any time she got up, for any reason, I looked at the couch for evidence that she may have been dripping. I wished vaginas were equipped with a high water alarms that sounded when moisture levels rose. Come to think of it, that would have had any number of awesome applications throughout my life.

It was Friday and it was time for yet another weekly midwife appointment, this week, we were meeting with Teresa again. I was worried about Ellen driving this far into the pregnancy, but it wasn't practical for me to leave work and pick her up. It would have taken all day, so instead I met her there just after lunch. Traffic was light, and I got there fifteen minutes early, which to me was dangerously close to late. Ellen was nowhere to be seen. I waited anxiously, watching the elevator doors open, revealing belly after belly, none of which were Ellen's. Ten minutes and three unanswered cell phone calls later, I began to worry. I daydreamed, vividly developing strategies to sneak a ceramic pistol through a court room's metal detectors, so I could shoot the Blackberry text messaging driver that probably killed my family. I decided that I would pull the trigger just as the not guilty verdict to vehicular manslaughter was read by the jury.

Finally, Ellen showed up, still pregnant and not dead, smiling across the waiting area as she walked up to the front desk. She checked in only minutes before her scheduled appointment, like it was nothing, like she hadn't deliberately tortured me. We waited for nearly twenty more minutes before the nurse called our name. Mid-day appointments were the worst; by mid-day the whole schedule was already running late. Still, if I wasn't a quarter of an hour early, I cursed every car and red light that slowed me along my way.

The nurse led us to our room and told us that Teresa would see us momentarily. Momentarily turned out to be another twenty minutes, and between the drive there and waiting in the lobby, I had already missed more work than I wanted to. Waiting was all I did, it seemed. I waited for my wife, waited for our baby, waited for our midwife, and waited to leave so I could get back to work.

"Well, hello. How's Momma doing?" Teresa asked as she walked in. She held Ellen's file out in front of her, where my head would be, so she saw only Ellen and the file.

"I'm good, I've been doing my yoga videos… and I know this might be silly, but I've also been doing some chanting exercises to try to help bring on labor," Ellen replied.

Teresa's eyes lit up, "O sounds are a great way to get the cervix to open. The cervix does as the lips do. I love when patients of mine chant. Even better, bring music into labor with you, something to help you chant during the delivery."

"We actually have an iPod, I can download some Tibetan monk chants for the delivery if that would help," I offered in an attempt to slight Daniel Day-Lewis while also persuading Teresa into lowering the clutched file that was continuing to block me out.

"That's great, getting into a squatting position and saying 'Oooooooo-Ahhhhhh!' is a great way to get things moving along." She lowered the file, re-enacting the position and sounds for us, "I love it when mothers and fathers are open to chanting. Keep it up and maybe we'll get lucky. I'm on call this weekend!"

I knew Ellen would love nothing more than to deliver on time, before the baby got too big, with Teresa. I was sure her enthusiastic O-face pushed her into a clear lead over the remaining midwives.

"I think I'd do well with you," Teresa added. "I think you'll probably withdraw into yourself. I tend to do well with people like that. You don't strike me as someone who'll drop a lot of F-bombs during labor. Not that that's a problem."

Teresa's observation was a good one. Considering all the times I had felt shut out by Ellen acting aloof. Finally some good might actually come of it. I couldn't imagine her screaming accusations like "You did this to me!" nor did I imagine her reaching out and squeezing various non-spongy parts of my anatomy. I was still concerned though, being a control freak, about having a silent wife during labor who would not communicate the important updates I would require. At least "Fuck you! When this is over, don't even think of touching me again!" hinted that she had the finish line in sight. Not to mention, she was still thinking of sex as an eight pound baby passed through her vagina.

WEEK 40:

YOU PART
THE WATERS

"**A**re you ready?"

How many times that week did I hear that question? My answer always the same, "Does it matter really? I think I'm going to be dragged into this regardless of how much I may or may not have prepared. I don't think I can call a time out."

People always laughed, "You're so funny! You're gonna be a great dad!"

I was just grateful that I wasn't a dad already. Surprisingly, Ellen's seemed just as reluctant as me, that was, until her mom arrived. I picked Karen up that Monday morning at the airport. She was excited to see me and questioned me the whole way home, asking about Ellen, the pregnancy and, of course, whether I was ready yet. Sigh.

We pulled up to the house and something felt different to me, almost ominous. Justifiably so, Karen's luggage hadn't even been dragged through the front entryway before I spotted Ellen. She walked out from behind the fridge door with a bowl, and mouth, full of diced pineapple.

"Mom!" Ellen yelled chomping down on a mouth full of delivery fuel.

"Ellen? What are you eating?" I asked hoping for any answer other than pineapple.

"Pineapple. I'm ready to have this baby," she replied.

Ellen went nuts that day, trying any and every natural induction method, which until now, we had painstakingly avoided. The next morning Ellen and her mom went to the *YMCA* so they could walk on treadmills and make "O" sounds before enjoying a pineapple breakfast. Her insanity continued; she took literally every action intended to spur on labor. That evening, she ate eggplant for supper while simultaneously applying self nipple stimulation. I remember walking into the kitchen and finding Ellen twisting her own nipples. At any other time in my life, this would have been a glorious moment, but not now. Now I was getting cold feet. Now it was watching her rev the throttle like Evel Knievel peering deep into the Grand Canyon, and I was riding bitch on the back seat of her motorcycle.

"Whoa!! Hold on... wait a minute..." I pleaded. "Let's think about this for a moment. We haven't even gotten everything ready yet. I can't carry all the crap scattered all over our bedroom into the hospital. If I am going to valet park, we need to consolidate. We need to completely re-pack. I thought we had an agreement? Are we still in agreement?" I asked rhetorically.

Ellen stared at me.

"What if your water was to break on the way? The car would sit for days in a parking garage with baby juice going sour on the passenger seat. That seat would cost me a thousand dollars to replace, money otherwise used for Abby's college fund! So I think you need to take a step back, let me wrap the front seat in trash bags, in the next couple of days we'll be ready to go. Can you please leave your nipples alone until then? Besides, Trina isn't even here yet and I couldn't possibly pick her up at the airport with a plastic covered seat. Don't you want your sister to be here for the birth? Who's going to pick her up if my passenger seat is covered in slick plastic? That's not safe! Okay, please, okay? No more treadmills, pineapple, eggplant, nipple stimulation, or sudden movements for a couple of days. Okay?"

"No," she replied defiantly.

It was the very next evening, late Tuesday night, when she realized she hadn't felt the baby move since her morning marathon at the "Y." We quickly grabbed the big jar of *Nutella*, pulling out a giant glob of chocolaty hazelnut goodness, hoping the sugar would give Abby a jolt of energy. Five minutes passed without any sign of movement. We were worried, we had been using this sugar rush strategy throughout the pregnancy to get Abby to move and, without exception, it had always worked. This was bad: I wondered if the umbilical noose had finally found its way around Abby's little neck. Or maybe she was in a diabetic coma from all the pineapple Ellen had been eating? Damn it! Maybe the *Nutella* just made it worse! I quickly grabbed the phone and called the midwife hotline, letting the middle-wife know it was urgent. Within fifteen gut wrenching minutes, our phone rang. It was Dot.

"Is Ellen in labor?" she asked.

"No," I answered, "but the baby isn't moving. Here's Ellen," I said as I tossed the phone to her clumsily, like a bee had just landed on me.

Ellen sat calmly, listening and answering questions that, judging by her answers, were clearly variations of "When was the last time you felt her move?" followed by "Could you have simply not noticed her moving?"

"James, can you get me a large glass of ice water?" Ellen asked.

I jumped up, ran to the kitchen and brought her back the largest glass of ice water I could pour in six seconds. It would have been nice to know that cold water could stir the baby to move, fifty thousand needless calories, spiraling towards gestational diabetes, worth of *Nutella* earlier.

Ellen drank the glass of water in less than a minute. This was no small feat for Ellen, who, unlike the rest of the animal kingdom, found remaining hydrated difficult due to water's offensive bloating effects. She sat silently with the phone pressed against her ear.

"She's moving," Ellen sighed with relief.

It was around midnight that evening that I had my first true run for the hills moment. Looking at the backlit LED clock on the dresser, I imagined grabbing my black duffel bag and vanishing into the night. Quietly tip-toeing my way through the house, collecting important things like Pygmy and... well, Pygmy. We would head north, using my Canadian passport. Maybe truck across Alberta into the wilderness just beyond the vast mountains of Jasper. Pygmy and I would live the rest of our natural lives in a log cabin, fat from eating the gamey tasting mountain rams. Most evenings we would cuddle up in front of a fire, wrapped in a ram-skin blanket. I would write in my journal under the flickering light of a ram-oil burning lantern while I swilled whiskey from a drinking horn made from, you guessed it, a ram's horn. But alas, Jasper was cold, and Pygmy and I were acclimatized to the Deep South. We probably wouldn't even make it through the first winter.

My truck wasn't even a four by four, and I hadn't driven in snow since I was a teenager. I'd probably skid off the road uncontrollably a day after crossing into Canada. Someone would find me two days later in a ditch, frostbitten, dead from the cold, wearing a hat that I had fashioned out of Pygmy. Back to Plan A: I needed to calm down, stay in bed, and quite possibly deliver this baby.

Both the midwives and Ellen warned me that this day would come. The day where once again my penis would be key to the pregnancy, but somehow I felt less like a sex machine and more like a surgeon. Tonight was going to be the night that Ellen would exercise her perceived right to force me, against my will, to have membrane-rupturing sex with her. I sat in front of the TV that evening, watching the minutes tick by on my DVR, knowing that as each digit blinked to the next we were moving dangerously close to the moment where my penis would become a scalpel. I imagined Ellen lying in bed with a big blue curtain draped across her waist. I wore a shower cap, a respirator from the garage, rubber gloves and an oversized tee shirt as improvised scrubs. Otherwise, I was bottomless with a bright yellow iodine-covered penis dangling from beneath my shirt.

Ellen got up from the couch; I was next to her watching television. "I'm going to go get ready for bed. I'll come get you when I done."

The last few weeks, my wife's desperate pleas for freedom from pregnancy had gone unanswered. Now, after almost forty-one weeks of enslavement, she had found her way out. Maybe I just needed an attitude adjustment. Maybe I needed to see this as an opportunity to be a hero. Technically, I was the only one with the ability to lead Abby and Ellen to freedom. I was like Moses thrusting his large staff into the air to part the Dead Sea. Sure, I didn't want the responsibility, but maybe this was the only way. Pineapple and eggplant could only take you so far. Maybe this was my penis' destiny. It wasn't some bloodied surgical instrument, it was God's tool, performing its own penetrating miracle.

Maybe Ellen would exit the bathroom in a linen robe and lay down on our bed as though it were an altar. A violent wind would pick up and the moon would immediately vanish behind the thick layer of cloud that had just blown over, the sky erupting with lightening as I walked towards her. My hair flapping wildly as I knelt in the center of the bed, reaching into the air with a roar, daring the night sky to dethrone me. With a powerful glare, looking down, mocking the Heavens' failed attempt to intimidate me, my miracle would begin. Lightening flickering like a strobe, wind growing ever stronger and the hail pelting down around us would be ignored. My daughter's freedom would come with a gush as the parting waters cleared her way. Unlike Moses, I would not likely remain dry, left behind in a puddle of nine month old baby soup with a checklist and a map to the hospital.

Ellen walked back into the living room and snapped me out of my divine fantasy. "Well, we don't need to have sex anymore. I think I may have just lost my plug, and no, I'm not leaking."

Huh, apparently the threat of my penis alone was enough to get things moving down there, not too shabby.

QUIET EYE OF
THE HURRICANE

I always thought that labor would be black and white. Though Ellen's cervix was open, and contractions had now begun, we were still at home. Everything we read and heard until now led us to believe that labor started and, magically, and within an undisclosed timeframe (less than two days and more than a minute) contractions would escalate to somewhere around five minutes apart. I was never given a good reason as to why we had to be so dangerously close to delivery before leaving. I assumed it was either to terrify the husband or allow the midwife time to grab a quick nap. More than likely it was the latter; labor almost always started at night. Although, parking at the hospital was hourly, so maybe it was to minimize the cost of parking. Either way, waiting was torture, and I would gladly pay additional parking if I could convince Ellen to leave.

Unfortunately, Ellen's labor wasn't black and white at all. False labor started on a Saturday night. Essentially, day one of week 41, and it crept up on us slowly as the week continued, like a predatory cat stalking her prey. The contractions were random, but got as close as two minutes apart. Ellen would hold her belly, breathe in through the nose and out through the mouth, requiring absolute silence. Once a contraction stopped, she would breathe a sigh of relief.

"Okay, it's over now," she would say as she exhaled.

Every night that week, we called the midwives around midnight. And every time we asked if it was time to leave for the hospital. They would vaguely suggest that it was early, but if we really wanted to come in we could. After careful deliberation, we consistently chose to try to gut it out and go back to bed. I was able to get moments of sleep through the night. Ellen got none, tossing and turning until dawn.

Every night, lying in bed, I thought "Tonight's the night!" Ellen was going to wake me up, and when she did, it would be our last night together alone for a very long time. Again, I would begin to panic. I didn't know which bag was which on our cluttered bedroom floor. I couldn't risk Ellen screaming for her socks during labor and not knowing exactly where to find them. I went completely blank. I forgot everything that Beverly had ever told me during those unfortunate birthing classes. What was I supposed to do during labor? If tonight was the night, it would be an epic failure. I couldn't even remember what exit I needed to take off the freeway.

C'mon James, you can remember this! I reassured myself.

I knew the most obvious exit led to a bumpy road, I couldn't take that one. I had to take the more obscure earlier exit, the less bumpy exit we discovered during the practice runs. I knew there was one road that Ellen got less angry on; later, she identified it as the optimal route, but only if I stayed out of the right lane. During one of our numerous practice runs to the hospital, I made the mistake of staying in the right lane. Every time I hit an undetectable dip in the road, which Ellen insisted only existed in the right lane, she freaked out. I may as well have been steering us deliberately off a mountain face towards the moguls on a black diamond ski slope.

"What are you doing? Change lanes!" she yelled, as if I had selected the "Trail Blazing" option on *Map Quest*.

"Baby, this was the way *MapQuest* told us to go. We can try another way on the way back," I replied.

"No! Change now, find another way," she ordered like the world's crappiest *Garmin*. What she lacked in British accent she made up for with bad attitude and no real direction.

I knew I should have skipped buying *Dexter* Season Three Blue-Rays and bought a GPS instead. Too late now, *Best Buy* was a no daddy zone. Anything bought in that place from this day forward would be regarded as the height of selfishness, robbing Abby of any possibility of a college education. All technology was off limits. My once state-of-the-art home was going to have to sit dormant for the next 18 years. I would become my father, listening to Crystal Gayle on an 8-track player while Matlock played in the background on our floor model television.

I woke up the next morning thrilled that Ellen hadn't gone into labor during the night. I immediately studied everything she had laid out, bags, maps, car seat. I even wrapped my passenger seat in black, yard-grade, plastic garbage bags. Each night I loaded the truck, and each morning I unloaded it again, leaving everything in the front porch, ready to go. This went on for the rest of the week while Ellen's false labor, which I dubbed as "abstractions", continued. By mid-week she was so exhausted from the contractions that any and all questions posed to her initiated a similar response.

"Baby, what are we going to do for supper?"

"Shhhh... I'm having a contraction," she whimpered while waving her hand and squinting towards the floor.

"Baby, where are the dogs?"

"Shhhh... I'm having a contraction."

"Baby, I've just been poisoned and Willie stole our diamonds. Where is the antidote?!"

"Shhhh... I'm having a contraction."

That Wednesday night was the closest we came to pulling the trigger. I had just picked up Ellen's sister at the airport on our recklessly slippery passenger seat, and within an hour of being home, our two female dogs and the three women brought estrogen to dangerously high levels. Strained from unloading Trina's luggage, I even caught myself leaning on a doorway with my right hand on my hip. Ellen's sister, Trina, was the final number in the combination to unlocking Ellen's cervix.

That night, the contractions grew stronger and closer together, and once again we called Dot, who had been on call for the second night in a row. It was clear from her tone that she was ready for us to have the baby. She too needed a single night's sleep without interruption. She told us that, though it was early, Ellen's reasonably calm demeanor between contractions sold us out. Again, if we really wanted to come in, we could. Otherwise, we should just make an appointment for the next morning. One of the midwives could check Ellen's cervix, thus avoiding early admittance.

As we waited in the office, the next morning, the nurse told us that Teresa would be our midwife. We'd had an intense week; hopefully Teresa would help us both relax. Ellen was so sleep deprived—she stumbled into the room like a post-apocalyptic zombie. Ellen's current state had totally convinced me that our midwife was going to lift Ellen's thin paper robe in horror. I expected her to be visibly startled by Ellen's dinner plate sized cervix, exhibiting a fluid-less uterus, and a stressed baby in need of immediate delivery. Instead, Teresa walked in, smiled, and casually completed her cervical check.

"You're about 3cm. You lost the mucus plug but I don't detect any leaking of your waters. Honestly, you haven't even started labor yet; these contractions are nothing but false labor. You need to go home, get lots of sleep and try and preserve your energy," Teresa said calmly.

Hasn't even started labor yet? I could tell by the inflection in Teresa's voice that "preserve your energy" was the key piece of information that we needed to walk away with. Ellen hadn't slept properly all week, and Teresa's casual dismissal of the contractions was alarming to her. If Ellen was this uncomfortable in false labor, she really needed to prepare for what was coming, and she knew it. This was a turning point for her, and for the first time during the pregnancy I saw that Ellen was visibly scared.

Unfortunately, the conversation didn't end there. Teresa concluded with: "Have sex this evening. If I was a betting woman, I would wager that I'll be seeing you again sometime tonight."

This was confirmation that it would be tonight. Teresa may as well have been Ellen's fairy godmother, offering her a single wish before the clock stuck midnight. This was exactly what Ellen had been waiting for, a way out. Her mom was here, her sister had just arrived the day before, and though she liked all the midwives, she had secretly wanted Teresa to deliver Abby for some time now. Tonight the car would not be unpacked.

Speaking of "full of baby stuff", it appeared my penis was coming out of retirement for one final dip in my wife's neonatal Jacuzzi. The mother ship's tractor beam was now focused on my shuttle. Already, I was fixated on the notion of a warm rush down my inner thighs as green baby poop infused biohazard gushed from the area surrounding my penis. I knew I wouldn't be able to do it; I would be permanently scarred if afterbirth engulfed my genitals, not to mention the physiological effects of lancing our baby through my wife's dilated cervix. Penis to baby contact was incest, and I couldn't allow it. My best chance for preserving my penis' innocence was in Ellen's contractions. As long as they continued to grow stronger, the last thing on her mind would be sex. All I had to do was remind her throughout the evening.

"Hey Baby, are they bad? That one looked strong. Is it getting worse?"

That evening was a long one. Ellen repeatedly leaned against any item of weight near to her as each contraction came. The contractions were always five to six minutes apart, as they had been all that week. The difference now was Ellen's reaction to them. She moaned and groaned through each contraction, and when they ended she needed the time to recover. Was this it? Was this the line in the sand? Because it felt more like it faded with every wave that swept over it. Every minute that passed made me feel like I would need to drive a little faster en route. Otherwise, Abby's passport was going to read "Front Seat" for her place of birth.

"Baby, I think we need to go," Ellen whispered.

"Click!" Like the sound of a gun cocking. That was the sound my brain made.

The scene from that moment forward would best be likened to a submarine dive. Ellen may as well have screamed "ALARM!!!" while sirens sounded loudly around us. I sprinted through the house collecting gear, tipping over lamps, and stumbling through the darkness. We were headed for deep waters. This wasn't a drill. If I had a pressure gage on my forehead, the little dial would have been well passed green, deep into yellow. And it was moving dangerously close to the little red bit on the far right. I hurried Karen, Trina and the dogs to each of their pre-determined muster points and gathered essential items, while sounding out everybody's role.

As predicted, we left for the hospital just before 11:00pm that same Thursday night. I did everything we had planned. I called Theresa and the hospital to let them know we were coming. I grabbed any remaining unpacked items that we might need, like our *iPod*, our *Bose* sound-dock, the flute, and the axe. The route to the hospital was followed with precision. I never changed lanes unnecessarily, and I entered each appropriate lane as soon as they became available. Christopher Columbus himself could not have plotted a more efficient combination of distance versus bumps. There was a distinct silence as we drove, like a terrified submarine crew listening for depth charges above them. The only exception, as was the case for all important moments in my life, was the soundtrack. "*The Insulation*" by *Menomena* played in the background. No one suggested I turn it down, or play something else, they knew my selection was deliberate. The melody and lyrics were specifically chosen to calm me as we drove. The memory would be forged in my mind forever when coupled with this beautiful song, always available for me to relive whenever it was played.

> *Begin to unwind, it's the process that's riddled with fear of mankind, the prospect of failing's on par with divine, there's a tip of an iceberg with wandering eyes, and sights set on melting a hole through your heart or a chute through the floor and my only request on your way out the door is that you take a bow.*

When we arrived at the hospital, I quickly abandoned my truck with the valet service and b-lined it through the lobby to the third floor. Like a dramatic TV doctor just called in for emergency surgery, I wasted no time. I confidently walked up to an intercom on the wall next to the locked glass door to the maternity center and announced our arrival. Karen and Trina looked baffled, like they were staring at alien technology. When it came to putting plans into action, my preemptive panicking always freed me of the burden of game day jitters. Under pressure, I was as steady as they come. If anything, I was so focused on the task that I was more likely to forget non-essential items like eating, blinking, and breathing. The attending nurse greeted us as we approached the front desk and asked us to follow her to our room: LD1.

"You're lucky; this is one of the best rooms. It has a window, Jacuzzi tub and a shower," the nurse explained as we walked through the door.

As we entered I wasn't thinking about the windows, the Jacuzzi tub or the shower. Instead, I realized I would be meeting Abby for the first time inside this very room. There was a spirit of joy in that place. I can only describe it as the opposite of a hospice, like they are both medical and spiritual yins and yangs.

As we settled in the room, the nurse helped Ellen into the mechanical hospital bed while demonstrating how to use it. She told us that Teresa had been called and that she would be arriving shortly. I wasn't interested in those details anymore: my mission of both notifying midwives and the hospital was complete. I had already transitioned into the role of coach. I was unpacking the bags, setting up the *iPod*, finding socks and snacks, and offering each of them to Ellen. I remembered everything! I imagined Beverly impressed. Despite not having a foreskin, I somehow managed to keep it together.

DAY 1:

BIRTHDAY

I t was about midnight when Teresa arrived. She quietly greeted Ellen and I, noticing that Karen and Trina had already laid claim on both the couch and the recliner. They were dozing off while I sat uncomfortably in the wooden rocker, exclusively placed near the bed to make husbands miserable. Teresa checked Ellen's cervix.

"Still 3cm, maybe 4," Teresa said calmly. "We've still got some work to do. Maybe we could run you a warm bath to help you relax?"

"I read that a lot of women use that when the contractions get more intense as a last resort. Maybe I could walk for a little since I still feel pretty good?" Ellen asked.

"Smart girl. But if you do that, I'm going to ask for an intense walk for about an hour," Teresa instructed.

Ellen and I found a quiet hallway off the main lobby near the elevators just beyond the locked door to labor and delivery. The area was crowded when we did the tour of the hospital. It felt completely different at midnight when it was empty.

There was no sense of urgency. Ellen became so relaxed that I second guessed our decision to leave our home, but just seeing the relief that fell over her when we arrived at the hospital was enough to convince me that we had made the right choice. We walked in circles through the looping corridor for nearly an hour. Steering from side to side, avoiding the doors with radiation warnings on them.

"How are you feeling, Baby?" I asked.

"Better," she sighed with a smile.

"You glad we came?"

"Yes," she answered sweetly, looking up at me.

After about forty-five minutes, we headed back to the room. Always the drill sergeant, I watched the clocks as we passed them, just to be sure we didn't miss our one hour follow-up cervical exam with Teresa. By the time we got back, she was already waiting.

"Still at 4cm. Let's go for another walk," Teresa said.

She wasted no time grabbing Ellen by the hand and leading us in the opposite direction from our previous walk. I started to sense seriousness in the air, like things weren't moving fast enough for Teresa. As we walked, she kept a fast pace between Ellen's contractions. When Ellen did stop for a contraction, Teresa would sweetly pull her hair back from her face until it passed. Each time, the passing contraction would immediately be followed by a series of questions about how it felt and where the pain had started. Based on the answers, Teresa would offer Ellen direction for the next one, like making noises and breathing more deeply.

Teresa led us through numerous halls and lobbies until we reached a sky walk with a stunning night view. It crossed the main street that passed through the medical center. The colorful lights from the surrounding skyline were surprisingly beautiful, for an otherwise understated view during daylight. As Ellen stopped for another contraction, a metro train passed below us. It looked like a completely different city, like somehow my perspective wasn't the same. I tried to think of the last time I had been out all night.

How did I land here? What lead me to this city, on this catwalk, with Teresa, the aging hippy midwife, and Ellen, my stunningly beautiful wife? She was the most beautiful woman I've ever dated, and now she was pregnant with my child. I thought of the small Newfoundland fishing village and how trapped I felt as a teenager. I wondered what I would say if I could send that kid a message. Deciding even if I could, I wouldn't. I had always felt like something great was down the line. I never lost faith. I truly believed God had a plan for me.

"Okay, let's turn around. We don't need you any more tired than you already are."

When we got back to the room, Teresa went in for another look.

"Okay, so here's where we are. Your cervix is nearer to 5cm than 4cm, so you're moving in the right direction and you are in active labor now, but at this rate, I think it's safe to say I will not be the one delivering Abby. Nina gets in at 8 am. I would try to rest as much as possible until then. When she gets here, I will fill her in on everything."

Nina showed up in our room by about 9:00am with our new nurse, Jayme. I was just waking up. Karen had generously gotten up off the couch just after Teresa left and let me catch up on some much needed sleep. Narcoleptic Trina was still out cold in the recliner. Karen took my place, uncomfortably folded in half, in the old rocker near the bed. Ellen hadn't slept at all.

Nina's arrival signaled me to go get food before the real work began. I got up from the couch and collected orders for *McDonald's*, which was located on the first floor. I never allowed myself to eat *McDonald's*, so this was going to be a glorious morning. Besides meeting Abby, what could possibly be better than an *Egg McMuffin* that had normal bacon substituted for the "Canadian" bacon, which, for the record, is known as ham in Canada. I took Karen's order; Trina was still sleeping and would inevitably ask me to go later, as she woke, at the exact moment Abby's head crossed the vaginal threshold.

By the time I got back to the room, Nina and Ellen were hard at work, transitioning from one birthing position to another. The giant training ball had been moved to the center of the room near the bed. Ellen was sitting on it, leaning forward over the bed rail for support. Horrified, I watched anxiously, waiting for a large squeak and clunk as Abby slid down the front of the ball landing on the floor. I fought every urge to ask if it was safe to be using this particular birthing aid this late in the game.

I could already tell that my role with Nina in the room was going to be significantly less active than it had been with Teresa. As a control freak, that was going to be a struggle. Not so much doing less—I was cool with that—but not being able to discuss the safety of each new birthing maneuver was going to be difficult for me. I leaned back in the rocking chair and asked if there was anything I could do before I started throwing back my modified

Egg McMuffins and super sized *McCafe Mocha Latte*. Their lack of response, which I was used to after years of marriage to Ellen, made it clear to me that I was free to eat. Definitely best to eat quickly, before the threat of being splashed by various bodily fluids ramped up.

It was late morning now and Ellen had been working pretty hard for what was nearly ten hours. As Nina moved her from position to position, it was hard to tell if Ellen was just exhausted from the pain of her intense labor or if this was a cumulative fatigue from the week-long false labor. I asked thickly veiled questions, so as not to discourage Ellen. Nina's answers demonstrated a degree of concern.

She hinted towards the two main problems I had initially feared. One, we had pulled the trigger too early. Two, Ellen showed up to the hospital already exhausted. But until that morning, we didn't have the knowledge to gauge what was real labor and what was false labor. What felt intense last Saturday was a blip on today's radar, and I didn't know what I should do to fix it. Should I ramp up my role as head coach? Maybe feed Ellen some *Gatorade*, punch some lockers and scream motivational nonsense?

Nina checked Ellen's cervix again, "Hmmm, 8cm: that's good. I think maybe we should get you in the shower to help you relax."

Our nurse, Jayme, walked into the bathroom and got the water to a comfortable temperature. Jayme was amazing. She never left the room beyond what seemed like bathroom breaks and grabbing supplies to replenish the room. She constantly kept a dialogue with Karen and me, but always with a quiet kindness that didn't distract Ellen. She was helpful in calming us, and in waking Trina, who immediately asked me to go get her breakfast. Instead, I opted to hand her a twenty and directions to the first floor.

"Okay, everything's ready," Jayme called from behind the bathroom door.

"James, come help me de-robe Ellen," Nina directed as she slowly walked Ellen to the bathroom.

Nina pulled the door closed behind us and rhetorically asked if I would be okay on my own for a while. By the time I answered, she had already walked away, glancing down at her *iPhone*, which I had noticed throwing out text messages and distracting her for nearly an hour now.

"How you feeling, Baby? Am I doing okay?" I asked Ellen as she tottered back and forth underneath the warm water.

"Better now that I'm in the water. You're a good coach, Baby," she reassured. "Where's Nina?"

"I'm not sure Baby, I overheard her and Jayme talking about another patient. I'm sure she'll be back soon."

She wasn't back soon. We stayed in the shower for nearly thirty minutes. Until I noticed pink fluid running down the inside of Ellen's leg. I poked my head out the door and instructed Jayme to let Nina know that Ellen was leaking fluids that weren't green.

"Okay. It's just a little blood, that's normal," Jayme replied.

Until now, Nina and Jayme had been so fast to yank out and replace disposable pads under Ellen's bottom that the whole delivery had felt remarkably sterile. There were none of the disturbing smells and viscous fluids that Beverly had spent so much time preemptively freaking me out about. Where was the thick yellow stuff and watery green stuff everyone cringed about uncomfortably in Beverly's living room? Why had Beverly spent so much time trying to turn my wife's beautiful vagina into some volatile, biohazardous fluid-filled flesh cannon with a forty week timer?

Jayme laid out a new pad on the bed, came into the bathroom, and helped me move Ellen back to the main room. She dressed Ellen in a fresh new birthing nightgown. Ellen refused to wear a hospital-provided gown. Instead, she had deliberated long and hard, trying to find "cute" nightgowns in which to give birth. I remember thinking how ridiculous it sounded. To me, it was like wanting a nice new suit to be executed in. Though, to be fair, that was more based on images in my mind of blood-drenched nightgowns being thrown around during labor like tissues from a nose bleed, an image I retained from our birthing classes. Obviously, Ellen was justified. The gown she had been wearing had made it for nearly thirteen hours. Even then, it looked fine to me.

It was almost noon, and I was ready to find out what Ellen's cervix was doing, but Nina hadn't returned. If only there was some new technology to give a real-time reading of the cervix. Some amber LED light that read like a thermostat on an industrial freezer in the form of a digital broach you could pin on the pocket of a woman in labor. "What's the cervical broach read? Ah... 8.34cm. You are coming along nicely." Unfortunately, this useful baby birthing technology had not yet been developed. Add it to my "to-do" list. The only indicator was evidenced by Ellen's intensified labor. I couldn't help but be impressed by how she gave no consideration to taking drugs while in such excruciating pain. Hell, she hadn't even asked me for a back rub, which was nice. I hated giving back-rubs.

"Baby, do you think you could give me a back rub?" Ellen asked. "Better yet, maybe Trina could give me one?"

Before I could turn around, Trina, a massage therapist, had already perked up and started on Ellen's lower back. This bought me some time to, frustrated, poke my head out of the room every two minutes to look for Nina.

I could tell Ellen was also nervous without Nina in the room, looking constantly at the door while we waited for her to come back. By the time Nina finally showed up, Ellen's massage had long ago ended. She quickly checked Ellen, making no excuses for her absence, but instead announced her decision to move Ellen into the bath tub. I began to feel like our delivery was a burden to Nina, and this was bothering me. I decided to stay out of the bathroom while Nina and Jayme coached Ellen. Best for me to settle down for a while; besides, there wasn't enough room for the four of us in the bathroom. I may as well let Nina earn her paycheck. Thirty minutes passed before Nina called me into the room to help Ellen get dried off. The tub was pink.

"Can you ask Mom and Trina to leave?" Ellen whispered as I walked in.

This was huge. We spent a lot of time discussing who should be in the room when Abby came. Beverly even went as far to say that whoever was there when the baby was conceived should be there at birth. This was a rare occasion where Beverly and I saw eye to eye. Karen and Trina begrudgingly left with the promise of being invited back shortly after the baby was born.

Ellen could barely walk to her bed. Nina and I helped her on her way back, but this time we didn't dress her. We pulled a blanket over her torso, leaving her bottom free for Nina. It was nearly 2pm, and after 15 hours of intense labor, it was almost time for Ellen to start pushing. She was in transition.

Nina began coaching Ellen on the most effective way to push. I could tell Ellen was holding back; she wasn't ready. Was she afraid of the responsibility, caring for a baby like I had been? Maybe she was just scared of the science behind it all, episiotomies, C-sections, epidurals and hemorrhaging? Ellen continued to struggle, and she wasn't consistently pushing the way Nina wanted her too. Every time Nina pushed on the area where she wanted to feel pressure, Ellen would do it, but within a few short seconds she would fall back to pushing weakly. It probably didn't help that every few minutes Nina was thumbing across her *iPhone*, insincerely repeating "Good girl, that's it," distracted by messages that clearly took priority over our baby's healthy delivery.

The pushing continued, as did Nina's distractions. Ellen was fading fast. The exhaustion from a sleepless week had chipped away at her both physically and mentally. On top of that, it was clear that we had pulled the trigger too soon and never should have come to the hospital so early. Over the next two hours, Ellen transitioned from standing, to all fours, to the exercise ball and everything in between, while Nina ducked in and out of our room. I even left the room at one point, so Ellen could focus without having to worry about modesty and me seeing any potential gore. By all accounts, I had seen nothing even remotely close. The whole thing was generally pretty soft-core compared to Season Three of *Dexter*, which I comfortably watched on Sunday nights while eating dinner.

It seemed as if the moment Ellen gained any confidence or strength to push, Nina walked out to play with her *iPhone*. When she wasn't, she was answering the call of nurses, who inconsiderately walked into our room and watched for several minutes before interrupting. Every single time, it resulted in Ellen staring distracted at the door while Jayme tried to keep her on track. Jayme was a rock star. She continuously did her best to echo everything Nina had been saying in her absence, except with sincerity. I was grateful we had Jayme, and I knew Ellen was, too.

Nina entered the room again, back from whatever emergency kept pulling her away. She looked at her watch, then told Jayme to go ahead and give Ellen a hep-lock. I knew a C-section was imminent, and Nina was worried about Ellen's tired uterus. She wanted to be able to get Pitocin in quickly after the baby came to help Ellen's uterus contract and reduce the risk of hemorrhaging once the placenta came loose.

What I didn't know at the time was that Nina had painted herself into a corner. By following Ellen's wishes to avoid almost any type of medical intervention, she wasn't in a position to call a doctor anymore without losing a lot of credibility. She had waited too long. Normally, this hospital's practice was to begin interventions after the first hour of pushing. We had past that point by over an hour. Nina took a position in front of Ellen's naked body. The blanket that had once covered her was now lost.

"Okay, I can see the head, it is very important that you push very hard. Once the head crosses the pubic bone, it will lock in position and no longer slip back. At this point, I will ask you to *stop* pushing. You hear me, you're almost done? You ready for one final push, Mamma?"

For the next hour, Ellen pushed so hard that her whole body turned purple. If you haven't pinned your wife against a bed like some Pro-Wrestler with one arm around her leg and the other around her head while staring into her straining naked blue-violet breasts, you may as well be strangers. I gazed between Ellen's legs at Nina and Jayme's reaction for nearly half of the sixty minutes. They repeatedly rose up in excitement only to collapse back down, discouraged and repeating "You are so close!", "She has so much hair" and "She's right there!" every alternating minute.

Again and again, the head moved forward. Again and again it slid back, not able to take the turn needed to cross the pubic bone. Abby was just millimeters away from locking into position. With each failing push, Nina stared at me with growing concern. She didn't need to speak, I knew we were on the bubble. Realistically, our bubble had probably had already burst. It was time for me to truly coach Ellen.

"Baby, listen, this needs to happen now. Do you hear me? It has been a long time and this needs to happen now. You need to push with everything you have, right now."

Ellen stared back at me. Even now she looked so beautiful, more beautiful than she had ever looked. I just wanted her to have the natural birth she so badly wanted.

"Baby, this is it, the un-medicated birth you wanted to have, no C-section, no Pitocin. But you have to do this right now."

Just as she pushed, another stranger interrupted by walking into our room. She began talking to Nina and, after a short discussion, again they both left.

"I really wish that would stop happening," I said to Jayme, clearly irritated.

"I think she has a breach birth happening now as well. She'll be back," Jayme replied. "Oh, so close. She was right there. You almost did it, Momma! Keep pushing!"

"Maybe we should wait for Nina to come back?"

Jayme and Ellen ignored me. I looked up at the clock: it was 4:30 pm. Ellen had been giving it her all for two and a half hours.

"Okay!" Jayme shouted.

"What?! Did it stick?!" I panicked. "Ellen, stop pushing! Should she stop pushing?!"

Jayme leaned back smiling, "Yep, look you can see her head right there."

I was almost too busy flashing between the door and Ellen. I looked at Abby, "Ellen, stop pushing!"

"I CAN'T!!!" she screamed.

I looked at Jayme in terror, "Nina said after the head crosses she's supposed to stop pushing."

"It's okay," Jayme said calmly looking down with one hand in Ellen's vagina. "Whoa! Okay, stop! Stop pushing!" she shouted abruptly, and immediately looked towards the door.

I jumped up and ran to the door, stuck my head out and saw no sign of Nina. I ran down to the front desk which was thirty seconds away. The nurses heard me coming. As I turned the corner all ten people at the front desk were staring to see what charging animal was about to appear.

"We need Nina now!" I said not quite yelling, but certainly not casually. "Baby's coming Nina or no Nina," I said while turning around and running back towards the room.

Ellen was still pushing when I burst back into the room.

"Try and relax," Jayme told her. "You're doing great," she repeated over and over.

For ten of the longest minutes of my life, Ellen and Jayme worked together while I stared at the door. The image of Nina casually tapping her *iPhone* had been looping in my mind. Nine months of planning, and now in the moment of our daughter's birth we had neither a midwife nor a doctor. I had imagined giving birth alone in our bedroom, in our yard, in the car, in the lobby of the hospital, and in a broken elevator in the hospital on the way to the third floor. The only scenario I hadn't planned for was a delivery without a midwife or doctor in a labor and delivery unit.

DAY 1:

AFTER BIRTH

"**D**o we have a baby yet?" Nina asked as she poked her head around the door.

Not funny.

"Almost!" Jayme replied.

"Great!" Nina said, visibly relieved.

Smiling, she peered into Ellen's vagina as she casually stretched on a new pair of rubber gloves.

"Look, Dad, I told you she had lots of hair."

As I looked down, I saw a single thick black curl, like Dr. Seuss' greatest creation realized right in front of me. It was the cutest little curl I had ever seen. I didn't see biology; there was no science experiment, no gore and everything else in the room truly dissolved around Abby's thick black curl.

The next few hours were made up of moments, individual clips like a highlight reel etched in my memory forever. Between those moments were nothing, people appeared from nowhere, Abby materialized from one location to the next. My mind couldn't keep up. After seeing her thick black curl, there was the moment when I saw her change colors from a bluish hue to a reddish pink while she dangled from Nina's hands. The next memory was the moment I saw Abby's tiny foot and the strange fleshy blister on the sole. Then, like she had teleported, I saw Abby against Ellen's chest. There were conversations happening around me like a bustling train station—white noise. Only a few direct questions would stay with me.

"Would you like to cut the umbilical?"

"No," I replied, lost in the vision of Ellen holding Abby in her arms.

"Are you keeping the cord blood?"

"No. Donate it please."

"Would you like to keep the placenta?"

"No."

Nina swept it into a bucket on the floor.

"What's that on her foot?" I asked.

"Huh, it almost looks like a sucking ulcer?" Nina replied.

It wasn't a sucking ulcer, it was the one hundred and fiftieth recorded case of a very rare disease called C.S.H.R., which could easily justify a book of its own. In the simplest of terms, it would be my largest test of faith and, annually, for the next eighteen years, when we undergo testing, I will be reminded to deeply fear its return.

"She's beautiful!" Trina said.

At some point, Trina and Karen appeared. I didn't even see them come in. Did I signal someone to let them in?

What was truly profound was the moment I fell in love with Abby. When Abby stopped being a word we used to describe the pregnancy, an abstract idea to me only moments ago, was now my little girl's name. Abby was my daughter.

I remember getting our pictures taken and the pride I felt for Ellen and Abby. My two perfect girls. Everyone said that Abby looked like me: such a simple statement made me so happy. Our only prediction was right, and Abby's long black curl was proof that she was mine. The pregnancy book told us that it was believed in Russia that if a woman had a difficult labor, the mother had lied about the father of the baby. Well, we were not in Russia, and Abby was unmistakably mine. Abby wasn't born in a manger, a hurricane or in the front seat of our car, but she was still a miracle.

Throughout the course of the pregnancy, I learned little about letting go of control. Yet in the moments of my daughter's birth, I realized that maybe I had never been in control at all. Despite how painfully hard I tried to be the perfect father, while preserving the perfect pregnancy for her, the truth never actually became clear until her birth. None of the details that I had worried so much about over the course of the last nine months really mattered. Abby would have always been perfect in my eyes from the moment I saw her.

She was the first impression of a pencil on paper, a dot before the beginning of a long line that could move in any direction. Throughout my life, lines had been all around me, and I had even seen a few end as the pencil lifted from the page. But until now, I had never seen a line from its beginning, making contact. That was what I felt, contact with something divine: she was innocent, perfect and sinless. I wanted every movement and moment in her line to be perfect. I wanted to keep her pencil sharp and her paper clean. That is my job, trying to help push her along in a straight line, and most importantly, be there for her whenever her line may smudge.

ABOUT THE AUTHOR

In his spare time, James Vavasour enjoys lifting the veil of untruths regarding the joys of pregnancy. He has successfully published several technical papers and magazine articles relating to offshore oil and gas. Most importantly, he recently survived a nine month long battle with pregnancy. These days, James and his wife joyfully fumble their way through parenthood with their beautiful daughter.

Get an Exclusive Sneak Peek of:

BirthCONTROL II:
A Husband's **Honest** Account of Fatherhood

Go to

www.birthcontrolthebook.com

and join the mailing list to be:

• Automatically entered in 1 of 12
monthly drawings for a signed copy of:
BirthCONTROL:
A Husband's HONEST
Account of Pregnancy

• Provided access to the
BirthCONTROL photo album

• Provided access to download
an exclusive sneak peak of:
BirthCONTROL II:
A Husband's HONEST
Account of Fatherhood

CPSIA information can be obtained
at www.ICGtesting.com
Printed in the USA
JSHW052154161120
9622JS00001B/99